T0194936

ENDORSEMENTS

for

Generating Learning Opportunities

"This book is a must-read if you want to see our future generation achieve success. The author weaves her knowledge and experience in a compelling manner that engages the reader in personal reflection. You close the book recognizing that your values drive your actions and these values are integral to academic success!"
—Patricia Larkins Hicks, PhD
President, Outcomes Management Group, LTD

"Glo absolutely hits a home run when connecting the value of life experiences, family values, and academic achievement to their influence on positive outcomes. This read will instill hope that any challenge can be overcome by this powerful combination. May you grasp this very valuable formula to generate life-learning opportunities."
—Dr. Kim Carter
Sr. Onsite Dean, Capella University
Owner and CEO, The Leader Igniter Group

"Gloria 'Ms. Glo' Redding has written a practical, must-read primer for anyone who cares about the future of children, families, communities, and the world. Read this book and learn from one of the best."
—Jo Hamilton, PhD, Executive Director
Digital Strategy, Design and Development, Laureate Education Inc.

"Glo's gift for relating to people through her family values and the passion she has in this area makes this book so important for anyone who wants to be a better parent, child, sibling, and leader in the community. Very practical how-to's from her personal and professional life experiences."
—Lashana Crone
HR professional and business owner/COO

"Glo understands the invaluable influence that the home has on a child's academic achievement. Throughout this book, parents will receive practical and proven methods that empower their children to succeed in life. Many families have benefited from Glo's passion and dedication, and she is committed to helping children reach their highest potential. While reading **G**enerating **L**earning **O**pportunities, parents will come away knowing that they are vital to creating the loving and nurturing home that is essential to their child's academic success."
—Ron Hitchcock, DMin
Marriage and Family Life Pastor, Vineyard Columbus

"This book not only practically explains how the value system into which young people are indoctrinated but is also an extraordinarily instructive guide. It acknowledges the foundation for academic and life achievement. Learn how to become a more supportive adult figure that instills these values by taking small actions each day. Every adult, be they parents, teachers, guardians, mentors, family members, or friends, will understand their power to positively impact life trajectory."
—Keisha J. Hunley-Jenkins, JD, PhD
1991 Young Scholar Inductee

"Generating Learning Opportunities: Family Values with Actions That Lead to Academic Achievement nicely integrates educational theory and practice with personal vignettes and stories. In my opinion, Gloria Redding has produced a book that is both practical and reader-friendly. Families, educational practitioners, and laypersons are destined to walk away from this book with many nuggets to apply with youth."
—James L. Moore III, PhD
Interim Vice Provost for Diversity and Inclusion and Interim Chief Diversity Officer
Executive Director for the Todd Anthony Bell National Resource Center on the African American male
Education and Human Ecology Distinguished Professor of Urban Education
The Ohio State University

"Glo tells her story with the type of authentic transparency that draws the reader in and demands introspection and transformation."
—Retired Judge Carla Moore

GENERATING LEARNING OPPORTUNITIES

Family Values with Actions
That Lead to Academic Achievement

Gloria Ann Redding

To order additional copies of this book, contact:
Xlibris
1-888-795-4274
www.Xlibris.com
Orders@Xlibris.com
723787

DEDICATION

Mary Ella Pride Mitchell

To my dear mother and best friend, whom I miss so much. Thank you for instilling a foundation of family values and encouraging me to always generate learning opportunities. You continue to live in my heart each day of my life. I love you, "Muva"!

I dedicate this book also to the following godly people who have passed through my life and encouraged me to always generate learning opportunities.

Mr. W. D. Watkins Sr.

Dad, you taught me foundational business principles and demonstrated the essence of a strong work ethic.

Mr. Roselle Mitchell

Dad number two, you were the gentle giant in my life who challenged me to think more deeply, be aware of my surroundings, and enjoy the journey.

Mr. Robert Moore

You were my father figure who offered academic support and demonstrated family values to a countless number of students at Buchtel High School in Akron, Ohio.

Dr. Janet E. Williams

My dear girlfriend and Delta Sigma Theta sorority sister, you and I were supposed to write this book together. When we met during our undergraduate years at The Ohio State University, it was instant sisterhood. We walked through academia, marriage, careers, children, and vacations together. Your demonstration of respect, patience, family values, and unconditional godly love to all you encountered was life changing for me.

Jacquie Matthew-Thomas

You often reminded me that, as Albert Einstein said, "We can't solve problems by using the same kind of thinking we used when we created them."

Dr. Debra Williamson

Family, friends, education, and music directed your path. Thank you for caring and sharing.

Theresa E. Wilkins

You were a multitasking servant for family, friends, education, career, Delta Sigma Theta Sorority, community, and God.

ACKNOWLEDGMENTS

God
"With God all things are possible"
(Matthew 19:26, New International Version).

My Husband
James W. Redding Jr. MSgt., USAF Retired, you allowed me space and time to think, write, and create while standing strong beside me as I completed this book. I will forever cherish your contribution and support.

My Children
Clifford Michael Cannon, you are the son who walked this journey with me every step of the way, and I thank you for allowing me to share our story across the pages of this book. As the child of a single mother, you stood with me during many difficult life tasks as we practiced family values and academic achievement. You make me so proud.

Leslie A. Cannon Jr., James Redding III (Jazz), Jennifer McCarter, and granddaughter, Celeste Naa Ama Cannon. I appreciate your love, encouragement and words of confidence, and I believe in your abilities and future.

My Siblings

My siblings, with whom I have shared a lifetime of love, include W. D. Watkins Jr., Ronnie Leon Watkins, Lucine Valrie, and Sandra Kay West.

All

My sincere appreciation to family, friends, community, tribe, and numerous others for your encouragement, support, love, and prayers along this journey.

SPECIAL THANK YOU
TO THE
GENERATING LEARNING OPPORTUNITY TEAM

To those who provided professional counsel, brainstorming, project management, organization, administration, proofreading other task, I sincerely appreciate your support, time and love.

Drs. Phil and Barbara Newman, Dr. Jim Bishop, Dr. Linda James-Myers, Retired Judge Carla Moore, Dr. Josephine Hamilton, Eric Troy, Yvette Alexander-Slate, Ryan Slate, Dr. Ron Hitchcock, Dr. James Moore III, Dr. Patricia Larkins Hicks, Dr. Carol Chinn, Martha Baker, Alexis Wilson, Derrion Harris, Alisha Clark, Gale Cornute, Vivian Tate, J.D., Dr. Kim Carter, Doris "Mama" Moore, Moms Geraldine Sims and Joan Jackson, Donald Lomax, Lucine Valrie, Sandra Kay West, Ruby Jackson, Chelsea Elliott, Dr. Keisha J. Hunley-Jenkins, J.D., Lashana Crone, Sandra Buckner, Terrye Wallace, Vickie Bradley, Zandra McEntie, Milton Little, Kristen Guest, Michelle Latting and Jordin Crone.

Alexis Wilson, I never thought that I would appreciate your daily prompts that pulled my story out and onto paper. You are such a gentle inspiration.

Joylynn M. Ross I offer you my gratitude for being my know-it-all, talented developmental editor and for continuing to provide my full service literary consulting and concierge service.

Lethichia Pope I am grateful for your commitment and daily executive administrative support. You are talented, timely, patient and amazing.

Aleatheia Mason owner of J&A Photography deserves photo credit for my professional back cover and the About The Author pictures. Thank you for being my "MemoryMaker".

I extend my appreciation to everyone who gave time, energy, knowledge, resources, or other assistance toward this book journey. May *Generating Learning Opportunities* serve as a constant reminder that family values with actions lead to academic achievement.

Ask and it will be given to you, seek and you will find:
knock and the door will be open to you.
—Matthew 7:7

I can do all things through Christ who strengthens me.
—Philippians 4:13 (King James Version)

CONTENTS

FOREWORD

Dr. Barbara Newman

As a professor of human development with over forty years of university teaching experience, I find it especially thrilling when one of my students reaches the point where she is ready to share what she has learned with others. I met Gloria Redding when she was a student in Human Development and Family Science at The Ohio State University. From the very first encounter I was impressed with her sense of purpose.

Gloria was balancing the demands of graduate school with her administrative role in the Young Scholars Program and her responsibilities as a single parent of a wonderful young son. Spending time with Gloria gave me insight into her background— neither of her parents had graduated from college—and into her passion for education. She was determined to complete her master's degree and to provide her son with the best education our community could offer.

There is no shortage of books that promise to enhance a child's academic achievement. But in this small volume, you will find a unique combination of life experience, professional insights, and practical advice that will inspire you to engage in the work of *Generating Learning Opportunities*.

Gloria weaves together the highlights of her life story with insights from research and effective strategies. She brings a new vision about how families can support their children's optimal development. Gloria speaks from her own life experiences, from lessons learned supporting working families, and from her years of work in corporate and educational environments. She understands what it takes to keep children engaged in the challenges of schooling. Gloria recognizes the frustrations that children and parents often encounter, and the essential role that families, friends, and mentors play in sustaining the commitment to educational goals.

A core theme in this book is the importance of family values that support academic achievement. Unfortunately, the term *family values* has become politicized; it has come to suggest a very narrow idea about families and their structure. In *Generating Learning Opportunities*, Gloria invites you to embrace a more humanistic view of family values. She argues for a scientifically based approach to parenting that incorporates appreciation for individuality, compassion, and group cohesiveness in an ethical view of family values.

For Gloria, family values emphasize affection, responsibility, respect, communication, and the determination to promote individual growth and personal fulfillment. These family values are foundational for inspiring the desire to learn, and the capacity to stay focused on educational goals. Gloria's message is right on target. She speaks out clearly, urging us to connect the dots between family values and academic achievement.

Families and communities need to be determined to provide the best possible educational experiences for their children. Fully functioning, loving, respectful, psychologically engaged adults are the secret ingredients to supporting a child's best chances for academic achievement.

Barbara M. Newman (PhD, University of Michigan) is a professor emeritus in the Department of Human Development and Family Studies at the University of Rhode Island. She has also been on the faculty at Russell Sage College and The Ohio State University, where she served as department chair in Human Development and Family Science, and as associate provost for Faculty Recruitment and Development. She has taught courses in life-span development, adolescence, family theories, and the research process. Dr. Newman's current research focus is on the sense of belonging among college students, with particular attention to students in minoritized groups.

INTRODUCTION

How can students, families, educators, and communities benefit from a concentrated incorporation of positive family values into their everyday living? For decades, both my personal and professional lives have involved education, family research, consulting, training, coaching, and family advocacy. I have interacted with students, parents, families, educators, and community members from coast to coast. These things combined have deepened my interest in the relationship between family values and academic achievement.

This book evolved from my direct experiences, which cover a great deal of ground. I do not attempt to tackle all the factors leading to successful families and academics, but I do identify common family values and actions that can support and contribute to academic achievement.

Much of my work has been with parents, students, educators, first-generation college families, and community resource providers to low-income families. I know that with help, drive, resources, and options, everyone can find a meaningful sense of purpose and success.

When we begin to pull back the layers of those things that are stumbling blocks on our journey toward academic achievement, at the core we will find the value system of the family environment into which we were born. The people by whom we were surrounded as we grew up and the journey we traveled with them have made us who we are today. That's how we learned the difference between right and wrong, good and bad, and acceptable and unacceptable.

Children quickly learn to recognize the voices of the primary adults in their homes, and those voices become the keys that monitor their behaviors. The primary adult's response to a cry or smile tells a child a lot about his or her world. A child's perspective on life is shaped by whether he or she is hugged, kissed, cuddled, or totally ignored.

We react to others based on our own individual personalities, and we form opinions and relationships as others assess us. One of our first lessons in life is educational as we learn to breathe outside the womb and then to eat, talk, and walk. Other survival skills soon follow. Beginning at an early age, we interact with adults in the home as students, forming relationships and establishing values.

Generating Learning Opportunities tells the story of my journey and the lessons I've learned about family values and academic achievement. I identify specific family values and actions that have been proved to be key foundations within many families.

I was raised in the Midwest in a strict, southern family where no meant no, yes meant yes, and children did not question adult authority. We respected our elders because, for the most part, we saw them as positive role models. I always felt loved, protected, and secure, so I developed an early appreciation for family and quickly began to model the values before me.

In the writing of this book, I candidly offer perspectives from my position as a daughter, sister, wife, stepdaughter, niece, aunt, mom, stepmother, and grandmother. The core of my life is committed to engaging and empowering families, educators, and communities, and I share the family values identified in this book as a possible foundation for life. I chose to document my journey as a small token of my gratitude to those family members, friends, neighbors, churches, teachers, mentors, and businesses who provided support along my pathway.

Throughout these pages, I've identified common family values, elements, and behaviors that support and contribute to students reaching their full educational potential. My desire is to help guide parents, caregivers, families, educators, businesses, and other community organizations through practical thoughts, suggestions, and ideas. Together we can work toward building a foundation of family values for desirable educational and personal life outcomes for all students. I believe that if we all work toward this goal, many unproductive societal challenges can be overcome and students will experience a positive effect and an optimal quality of life.

I invite my readers to consider the following positive family values: respect, dependability, responsibility, self-sufficiency, assertiveness, and a strong work ethic. Also, determine where you can take actions that contribute to and encourage love, communication, high expectations, parent involvement, and daily homework.

My intention is in no way to judge anyone's family values or parenting skills. Instead, I offer information, hope, and praise to help reinforce, support, and encourage you in your own family and educational arenas. A few small but powerful adjustments to family values and actions outside of school could lead to economic empowerment and flourishing individuals, families, and communities, as well as cities full of academically high-achieving students.

To gain the most from this book, read it while reflecting on the current relationships in your life. Although we know that each family and child is different, please think about what family values have already worked for you. What stories do you have to share? This may require some self-reflection. Ask yourself, "How can I most effectively engage and empower the children in my home, family, or community?"

I know that many readers can relate to the values and experiences shared within the pages of this book. While reading, find a place where you can identify your role as a generator of learning opportunities.

Below are some general definitions that will help you navigate the book. For introductory clarity, the terms below will serve to direct our path through *Generating Learning Opportunities*:

- **Value**—a desirable standard, principle, or behavior by which to live
- **Family values**—the standards, traditions, moral principles, goals, and objectives learned, shared, or enforced by a group of people who occupy a common residence or are closely connected—often related by marriage, birth, adoption, or guardianship
- **Academic achievement**—the level of successful education or knowledge gained as shown by scholastic testing, knowledge demonstration, or performance assessments

This book was designed to generate learning opportunities based on family values and easy, everyday actions in the home that can lead to academic achievement and prepare students for our evolving, diverse world. I hope you find that it accomplishes just that.

PART 1

Family Values Lay the Foundation

Family Values Lead to Academic Achievement

Respect
Dependability
Responsibility
Self-Sufficiency
Assertiveness
Strong Work Ethic

CHAPTER 1

Family Values

Family is the place where people care
enough to uphold family values.
— Gloria "Glo" Redding

A family group may include parents, grandparents, caregivers, siblings, aunts, uncles, cousins, and sometimes close friends. Group members may be related by birth, marriage, adoption, or guardianship. Most core family members occupy a common residence.

Today, an escalating number of young adults ranging in age from eighteen to thirty-one, referred to as *millennials*, continue to live with their parents because of economics and a decline in the number of early marriages. Also, as elders live longer because of improved diets, health care, exercise, and overall lifestyles, more of them are living with their children. When I was a child, my extended family lived in another state and we saw our grandparents mostly during summer visits, but our relationship with them was strong. When I think of my grandparents, however, the word *respect* immediately comes to mind, and I would have welcomed them to live with our family.

As noted in the introduction, a value is a moral and ethical principle that provides structure to our lives and guides our decisions. Successful families pattern their lives, businesses, and careers upon personal values, beginning with respect for parents and other people within one's own living space. Being respectful means being dependable, responsible, trustworthy, and honest, and developing good relationships. When our expectations of one another are clear and uncompromised, life flows more smoothly for the entire family. Achieving this requires clear, concise, and tactful communication among the family members.

Family values form the core of our society and take many forms. What we all say and do is swayed by our deep core values, which are associated with many people, things, and life situations. I view the family as an organization to be operated like a business, which means there should be a manager. It is always a good family management practice to review your own family values, because every decision made within the family unit will ultimately affect the entire family, even if it pertains to only one person's direct actions.

As you look at your own family values and organization, do not get discouraged if certain areas seem to be lacking. All families have the choice to rebuild life and promote their own sense of what is important to them.

It is important to establish consistent basic family values before a child enters school. Basic foundational family values are the core things that a person believes—what *really* matters. I hope that you are reading this book because you believe in family and academic achievement and that you're looking for ways to generate learning opportunities.

I often talk with parents who appear amazed when their child misbehaves in school, despite being fully aware that their child has been lacking effective discipline at home. It's as if a parent trusts that their child will have the good sense to not misbehave outside of the home, even though they misbehave inside the home.

Think of it this way—before walking out the door, a child is handed a good behavior mask and is instructed to "act like you have some sense in public." That doesn't mean they are going to leave the mask on until they return home. If children don't respect parents and other family members in the home, it is unlikely that they will respect teachers or other adults in authority.

Parents are expected to offer support and encouragement for the family members in their home, especially the children. The more that parents' values are clearly defined and demonstrated, the higher the propensity of the child to adopt the parental value.

What are some ways you have defined and demonstrated values in your home?

_____

_____

_____

_____

What are some values you may need to work more on defining and demonstrating in your home?

_____

_____

_____

_____

Family Values Team

I believe in identifying a dependable support group of people who share mutual family values. These are the people with whom I share my life. This is my team to whom I can pass the ball, assured that they will respect my vision. My starting lineup was my mom and dad.

W. D. and Mary E. Watkins Sr. experienced my birth on April 4, 1952, in Courtland, Alabama. I grew up in a working-class family with a stay-at-home mom. When I was two years old, my family moved to Harriman, Tennessee and at the young age of four we relocated to Akron, Ohio. I understand now that Dad thought it was in the best interest of his family to move from the South to the North. In the 1950's some considered Ohio a land of liberty that provided more opportunities for African American families. An unwavering value of Dad's was taking financial responsibility for his family.

From my preschool years to my early adulthood, my family shared a unique, workable, and successful economic system that provided security and comfort. Ultimately, our family grew to include Dad, Mom, and my two brothers and two sisters. Family values were our solid foundation, and naturally embedded in us beginning at a very early age.

I first learned our basic core family values, and more complex lessons followed. I will share more about the specific family values I learned, in hopes that you, too, teach your own family-values lessons right along with your everyday routine.

Let's take a look inside the Watkins home, where we see Mom in the small kitchen with one big window overlooking the backyard. The olive-green and sky-blue dishes were stacked on our small, old, lopsided appliances. The table sat only four, so we pulled up an extra chair to seat all five children. Mom rarely sat at the table with us because there was no room.

The only time we saw Dad was on the weekends because of his work schedule. Even when he was home, he never sat at the dinner table. He always ate in the living room on a metal folding tray, sitting in his favorite chair in front of the television. He was always between jobs and had little time for talking, and he was barely able to fit eating and sleeping into his busy schedule.

Mom would often eat after the children, but she was active in our table conversations. She valued a clean kitchen, so all after-dinner activities were postponed until the kitchen was sparkling clean. Mom cleaned as she cooked, so most of the pots, pans, and cooking utensils were washed and put away before the meal. The tiled floor stayed swept and clean, a chore that was typically disbursed to the girls.

We learned many valuable lessons around those green-and-blue dishes, which were so sturdy that I can't recall any of them ever breaking. They must have been a status symbol, as we became a blue-collar working family. Everyone in the neighborhood seemed to have those same dishes. Some sets were sky blue and others were Christmas tree green, but they all had the same flowery pattern on a white background.

After supper and once the kitchen was cleaned, if time permitted, we kids would watch our newly purchased black-and-white, nineteen-inch Zenith television. It sat on the kitchen counter, so we would pull the kitchen chairs over to the counter and huddle around it. That was our final treat for the evening before heading upstairs to get ready for bed.

Our home had only two bedrooms, which meant close quarters for a family of seven. My parents had one bedroom, of course, and I shared the other, smaller bedroom with my four siblings. Five kids in one rather large, high, oak bed with a huge headboard wasn't the most ideal situation, but it was what we had. We were grateful, but that didn't mean we were comfortable. The three sisters slept at the top of the bed, and our two brothers were at the bottom. There was just enough room if some of us kept our legs straight and others slept in a fetal position.

In our home it was challenging enough to sleep with a set of toes in your face, so thank goodness Mom made certain that hygiene was a valued priority for us all. At bedtime one would often hear "Don't touch me," "Stop," or "I'm going to tell." To sleep peacefully, we all had to learn to value boundaries and respect.

Mom was always really big on family Sunday dinners, because she valued the family being together, especially on Sunday. She'd start preparing on Saturday—greens, ham hocks, fried chicken, golden-brown creamed corn, sliced tomatoes with vinegar, potato salad, and cornbread was one of her favorite meals to prepare for her family. For breakfast that day we'd eat Cornflakes and bananas with milk, which was just enough to tide us over until the Sunday feast. As good as breakfast was, I'll admit that it was hard to swallow, literally and figuratively, with the scent of the upcoming feast wafting through the air.

We had Neapolitan ice cream every Sunday, even in the winter. My siblings and I dreamed all week about the food that Mom was going to serve up for Sunday dinner. I believe that what Mom valued most was just the fact that our family was together and enjoying her tangible and tasty way of saying, "I love you."

In Mom, we saw dependability firsthand. No matter what was going on in life, we knew that she wanted us to all be united in love. Our family would eat, talk, laugh, sit in the backyard, relax, and simply feel a sense that we were important to Mom, who was our foundation. She showed us that she was committed to our family, which gave me motivation and inspiration to obtain my goals. It became natural for me to show my appreciation by excelling in all that I did, because self-respect, dependability, responsibility, and representing our family well were family values imparted early.

Christmas and Easter photo shoots were always a big deal in our home. We would get dressed up in new clothes that had been hanging in our closets for weeks. The anticipation of sliding into them and taking in the new-clothes scent would finally came to fruition. A professional photographer would come to the home and pose us in various positions—a step beyond today's selfies taken with cell phones.

The photos were always so funny, posted up on the mantel to display our family pride and unity. They have brought laughter and memories when the Watkins children have gotten together over the years. One can seldom walk into a home today and see family portraits. If you don't have your own family portrait, consider creating that experience. There is something about a family portrait that creates a sense of belonging.

Glo, Mom, W.D. Jr. and Dad

Lucine, W. D. Jr., Ronnie, Glo, Sandra Kay

Lucine, Mom, Glo and Sandra Kay

CHAPTER 2

Teaching Family Values

My family values generated learning opportunities
with actions that propel me through life.
—Gloria "Glo" Redding

MOM "Muva" - Mrs. Mary Ella Pride Mitchell

Family Values Taught by Mom

Mom was not only our family manager but also the family organizer, planner, and spokesperson. She was the second of nine children, all of whom had the same gentle, life-focused temperament and family values. She knew how to make friends, support others, and take care of home. I learned a great deal about God and life from Mom, and I can't imagine what my life would have been like without her. She provided emotional security and emphasized time management.

We didn't have an overflow of financial resources, but we were taught to carry ourselves respectfully. Mom always said, "No matter how much you have or have not, your clothes should be clean, because you are Mary and W. D.'s children—the Watkins kids." She always said it with such pride, which only confirmed the last part of her statement: "We take pride in ourselves and our accomplishments."

Pride and accomplishments became more than just words—they became values. They became actions embedded in us by our mother, to always be decent and clean. We weren't representing only ourselves, but our entire family unit. Mom's maiden name was Pride, and we were taught to take that name seriously and literally.

Mom never just assigned chores; instead, she took the time to teach us the art of cleaning. She would demonstrate the proper and most effective techniques. Then she'd allow us to do it ourselves until we got it right, even if that meant making a bigger mess in the process. I must admit that some of us became little neurotic cleaning freaks on many a Saturday morning, making our home immaculate for the upcoming week or just in case company stopped by.

Those early family tasks taught us responsibility, dependability, and leadership skills that positively affected my life. I felt pride in completing a task, such as washing dishes, making the bed, cooking a meal, or sweeping the dirt in the front yard, where for a long time we didn't have grass. That was the beginning of my deep-rooted core family values. However, not all of our neighbors had the same values when it came to cleanliness, which affected our living environment.

We learned an important family value through an awful childhood experience with roaches. Our home was the hangout for all the neighborhood kids, who knew that Mom delighted in cooking, baking cookies, and providing Kool-Aid for our playmates. My friends felt the overflow of love in our family, which was an example of sharing. But Mom didn't expect some of the neighborhood kids to share their pest problem with us.

Upon discovering that the little brown critters had been deposited in our home, Mom became very assertive. She rearranged the budget to find the funds needed to schedule an extermination service visit. We had to make sacrifices in other areas, such as clothing, snack food, and going to the drive-in movie. Living with roaches was something we never wanted to deal with again.

Seven of us in the home was plenty—we didn't need any extra, uninvited guests. As a result of the roach problem, we developed a heightened responsibility and depended on each other's efforts to maintain a bug-free home, in which assertiveness and dependability worked hand in hand.

Shortly after that experience, Mom, who pretty much handled the finances in our home, once again arranged the budget while Dad took on overtime work. This time, her financial savviness enabled us to relocate to the west side of Akron, which was our last move as a family unit.

Our new dwelling was a larger, red-and-white house with three bedrooms. It was in a healthier neighborhood as well, with enhanced home value where people took care of their yards. The streets were clean and safe. Schools were invested in the children and kept the parents informed. Shopping was easily accessible, and the neighbors respected each other.

Our house seemed to stand out from the others on the block, mostly because of the five active children who were always bustling about. I loved our new home, and as a child, I realized that money was what allowed my family to change our living environment. In my opinion, that was real-life financial education.

I started to focus my attention on school, and I appreciated the new environment and knowing that I was learning more. I felt better about myself and my future, and I was motivated to get more out of life. My parents were trying to show me the connection between education, work, and quality of life way back when, but I didn't connect the dots until later in my adult life.

My dear mother's actions taught me the value of being a dependable, responsible, trustworthy person. She lived and demonstrated the fruits of the Spirit: "But the fruit of the Spirit is love, joy, peace, patience, kindness, goodness, faithfulness, gentleness, and self-control" (Galatians 5:22–23, New International Version).

The family relations and human development focus that is part of my core value system originated from my mother. Working as a team with Mom to plan meals was a common occurrence at our home. I often had the job of shopping, cooking, or cleaning, and she always encouraged me and offered to teach new skills as I demonstrated more responsibility.

As I watched the way Mom managed the home, I noticed that she was witty in her technique, and little Glo always wanted to help out. Caring for five children called for both time management and planning, and Mom assigned us a task each day. She used the kids and our friends to assist whenever possible. We raked leaves, shoveled snow, sorted clothes, and dusted furniture. Often

Mom made it feel like a party for everyone who wanted to join in the fun.

As far back as I can remember, sitting still was always a challenge for me because of the excitement of helping Mom manage things. I recall standing in a chair at the kitchen sink with apron strings doubled around my waist. I had to have been maybe six years old, and my task was to wash dishes. Water was all over the floor and suds were everywhere, so Mom put newspaper on the floor to help sop up the water. Looking back, I wonder if Mom really needed my help that much or if that was her way of teaching me responsibility.

We spent many hours around the wooden kitchen table, just talking about family values and life as Mom held her coffee cup. Of course, back then I didn't label the subject matter "family values." It was when I began to mature that I realized that every story Mom shared had a life lesson incorporated with family values.

Mom was always eager to share with her girlfriends the things she'd taught me. I knew when she had been bragging on me, because when I saw her girlfriends, they would smile, praise me for my latest achievement, or pat me on the head. A mother can tell her children how proud of them she is until the cows come home, but when others relay those same sentiments, it's further confirmation. It is one thing when Mom offers encouragement, but there is something about the child knowing that she's telling others—and they are equally proud—that adds a louder ring of truth.

I attached to my mother's warm embrace early in life. When I learned a new task to help her, I became so excited that my heart would beat faster as I waited with anticipation of her approval. I wanted so badly to make her proud of me because she was a great mother and mentor, and I valued our relationship.

Mom was firm in her requests to her children, and we knew that her words grew out of protection and love. She built our foundation not on her educational background, but on these family values and goals:

- Look within a child and have a real desire to help them become successful.
- Seek resources in the family, school, and community.
- Remember that each child is different.
- Invite God to direct your path.

Without the slightest doubt, my most painful experience was the loss of a wonderful, loving, kind, beautiful, southern, Christian queen whom I call "Mom." But before she left this earth, she did an excellent job of instilling family values into my life, values that I am able to pass on to others.

Mom's voice still speaks to me today like a peaceful wind in my ear, or the feeling of someone squeezing my hand so tightly that it makes me smile and show all my teeth. Like Mom, I embraced the concept of helping people, gathering information and resources to generate learning opportunities based upon sound family values.

Family Values Taught by Dad

Dad commonly held two or sometimes three jobs to adequately provide for his family. He was employed at the B. F. Goodrich rubber factory and the US Post Office. He was involved in his postal employees' work community as an officer, and he was president of the local postal union chapter. Dad never wanted Mom to work, so she took on the duties of a stay-at-home wife, making certain that he had laundered work uniforms that represented self-respect. Providing for his family was a task Dad took seriously, and he was an outstanding example of a hard worker as he provided for his family of seven. His work was a driving force, and while he was taking care of business, he didn't have time for a personal relationship with his family.

Our father possessed skills to repair almost anything. *Remodel* could have been his middle name. He was self-taught, assertive in learning, committed, timely, and dedicated to excelling on every job. Teamwork was second nature to Dad, as he displayed when he purchased rental property to rehab. He would pull together a team of friends, associates, and business partners who had the skills to assist with getting the work completed. He always modeled a positive work ethic, and he taught us the importance of responsibility and making an honest living.

Dad had his flaws, though. No parent—no person—is perfect. There was a force deep inside him that eventually became so powerful that it divided our family. I remember police officers coming to our home as a regular occurrence. One night, Mom's dependable children all rose to her defense and fought valiantly to protect her from what would today be called domestic abuse. Unfortunately, as young children, we learned to be assertive in a confrontational manner against our own father. Mom was fortunate that her children were there to protect her many nights. In the sixties, police in our neighborhood did not get involved in domestic violence, showing up merely as an act of duty.

Dad taught me basic business principles and valuable workforce skills, which were the primary family values that he instilled in his children. I learned a great deal from Dad, and I'll always remember the strong work ethic he taught us.

Family Values Leading My Journey

The priority that I placed on my family values shifted as I grew from a small child to a teenager to a young adult, wife, and mother. The world could have easily caused me to rethink my deep core values of respect, dependability, responsibility, self-sufficiency, assertiveness, and a good work ethic. Things will occur in life that will put our values to the test and throw us off track. I haven't always stayed true to my values, but I've always known how to ask for forgiveness, grace, and mercy. I've always gotten up, brushed myself off, jumped back in, and continued the journey. Family values don't easily change after they become part of who you really are on the inside.

Today I am a sum of everyone, everything, and every experience in my life since childhood. I recall all the do's and don'ts, and there were words that we dared not say, things that we weren't to share outside our family, and places we could not go. I have shared valuable moments with Mom and Dad, my siblings, neighbors, people at church, school, and within my community—all of whom make up my tribe.

When I hear the words *family values*, I reflect upon my parents teaching and preparing me how to live with my family members, but also how to be productive at school and in the classroom, where family values were also to be displayed.

I still honor the values with which I grew up. At times they might seem *old school*, but they certainly worked back then—and they have endured the test of time. Here are some family values that I recall from my youth, which can still be assimilated into our everyday routines.

1) Sunday school class: This was an extension of school. Everyone at least appeared to accept the importance of living out family values.

2) Report card grades: Education was demonstrated by commitment to schoolwork. Mom never compared her five children or their grades. Her words were "Just do

the best *you* can." This was our preparation for academic achievement.

3) Cleaning the house: Pride and respect for our personal belongings and those of others could be seen throughout our home.

4) Braiding my own hair: Mom took pride in how her children looked, but with three girls, she felt that we should be responsible for our personal grooming at home and in school.

5) Big sister family tasks: I learned the responsibility of leadership and organizing through those Saturday morning household tasks.

6) Sports track victories: I learned assertiveness by competing in track, which required commitment and dependability.

7) Completing a sewing project: I took considerable pride in designing and sewing many of my own garments.

8) Babysitting: As a young teenager, I proved to be responsible and dependable with the care of children. Those entrusting me with their children recognized my family values.

9) Celebration of career success: No success was overlooked, and every accomplishment was a reason for celebration.

Although our family was a loving one, our parents' lack of cohesiveness had the possibility of affecting my academic focus, marriage life, and family values. However, no matter what happened, Mom refused to allow adult family matters to interfere with her children's academic achievement and her expectations of us. Daily homework was always a priority, no matter what was going on in the home, and there was always open communication. But most of all, there was love.

Mom kept the lines of communication open about school as she questioned us in detail about our day. Her expectation for our schoolwork performance remained high, but we were allowed to enjoy life as normal children. As much as possible, Mom shielded us from much of the family dysfunction and allowed us to be kids while her love radiated above all.

Family values can sometimes be strengthened through adversity, while very important priorities are adjusted and new problem-solving lessons are learned. Our family values reflect who we are and how we parent. When parents articulate and live by those values, their children learn life lessons. Their children learn to express themselves, solve problems, grow from mistakes, and develop other skills and abilities that lead to fulfilling lives.

Are your current family values in agreement with what will benefit the young people in your home or community? Are your actions leading to academic achievement? If not, it is my desire that within the pages of this book, you will find ways to ultimately answer in the affirmative.

CHAPTER 3

Family Values Lead to Academic Achievement

Your beliefs become your thoughts.
Your thoughts become your words.
Your words become your actions.
Your actions become your habits.
Your habits become your values.
Your values become your destiny.
—Mahatma Gandhi

For a student to successfully survive in a school environment while facing family adversity, they must be internally driven and able to overcome obstacles. Regardless of the family situation, children accomplish more when their parents have established positive family values and are engaged, consistent, and firm in their parenting.

Respect, dependability, responsibility, self-sufficiency, assertiveness, and a **strong work ethic** have been identified as key family values that lead to academic achievement. The definitions of the family value terms below will add clarity along our way toward generating learning opportunities.

Respect—To respect someone is to think highly of, admire, or have high regard for them as a result of their personal qualities, abilities, or achievements. Respect can be seen in how people perceive themselves and treat others as they would want to be treated.

Elders in my life earned our respect. We even feared them because they were so highly honored and valued for their age, wisdom, and knowledge. As youth, our communications with elders were always "Yes, sir" and "Yes, ma'am," while looking directly into their eyes and standing up straight with shoulders back in a humble, attentive posture. The elders in my circle of family, friends, neighbors, church, school, and community were engaging and empowering. They wanted to see me be successful and accomplished, having improved upon the life that I was leaving behind.

Some may say that plenty of respectful kids show no ambition in school. The two aren't necessarily connected, but behavior in an academic environment begins with self-respect. Only then can a student respect people of authority or their own classmates. Students encounter enough distractions without having to encounter the disrespect of others, which can be discouraging and have a negative influence on academic achievement, goals, and dreams. Parents can help limit distractions by making certain that teachers are aware of their academic and behavioral expectations for the student, while keeping in frequent communication.

In our tribe, all young girls were offered unsolicited advice on self-respect from well-respected women. We were schooled on everything from clothing choices to skirt lengths, hairstyles, and lipstick colors, which was their way of trying to keep us focused on school.

Dependability—Dependable people can keep promises, are reliable and trustworthy, can be counted upon, and are faithful. They tend to develop good relationships; engage in school, work, and play; and follow through on a task. I can still hear the words of my mom ringing in my ear: "I want to trust you to do what you say." This has been my guiding light in life.

Responsibility—Being responsible means accepting control, being accountable, providing leadership, and/or possessing authority. Responsibility can be seen in how one makes decisions for one's own actions. Responsibility for their own academic achievement should be one of students' first big personal assignments. How seriously a student takes and manages their own classroom behavior, class work, and homework will determine their outcome. Parents and teachers should consider cognitive abilities and age-appropriate tasks throughout the educational process at every stage of learning. It is helpful to begin this practice early in life with minor tasks such as picking up toys and clothing. This early start will give a child plenty of time to practice personal self-care and will guide their ability to take responsibility and excel academically.

Self-Sufficiency—Self-sufficient people possess great confidence in their own ability, value, and importance, and they require limited support, aid, and direction. Self-sufficiency can be seen in how a person obtains resources, tools, and networks—asking for assistance as necessary—to reach a goal.

Assertiveness—Assertive people act confident, self-assured, and determined; they possess the ability to stand up or advocate for themselves in business and personal relationships. Assertive people can speak to others in a positive, nonthreatening manner. In their relationships, they maintain a we-can-all-win attitude based on effective management and communication techniques.

Learning to use assertive behavior in a productive manner can be a real asset, because it helps you stand up for your point of view while maintaining respect for others but not being easily swayed. Developing communication that effectively balances aggressiveness and assertiveness takes practice. Communicating either harshly or in a threatening manner can be stressful; instead, we want children to be assertive and respectful, and to speak up in a confident manner.

Good Work Ethic—People who believe that work is a beneficial and moral responsibility have a good, strong work ethic. They place high value and importance on always doing their best job, and their determination to do so can often be observed in tasks and projects at home, school, or work.

As a child, I always kept an eye open to the professions of my family members, even though talk about adults' jobs between elders and children was not part of normal conversation within my circle. However, the elders always expressed how they wanted younger people to get an education, have a solid career, and increase their job options. It is a good practice for parents to share their work world with children of any age, because it can help mold a good work ethic, strengthen their character, and build integrity.

GOALS

Now I'll take a moment to discuss the importance of setting goals. Setting goals is a basic component of self-sufficiency. People who have a life plan and know where they are going are more confident, which helps them stay focused. It is helpful for a self-sufficient person to have effective goals that include components of the SMART acronym, which is explained in more detail at www. edutopia.org/blog/smart-goal-setting-with-students-maurice-elias as follows:

S = specific
M = measurable
A = attainable
R = realistic
T = timely

Family values and parenting are seldom discussed in a related context; however, my experience has shown that they fit like a hand in a glove. Together they are the glue that holds a family together, because parenting decisions should be based on smart family values.

Sometimes we may see parents who appear to be unconcerned and have no interest in family values or their children. The kids may be untidy and come to school unprepared or even sick, and the parents may spend little high-quality time with them. What we see might not represent a lack of family values, but evidence of financial, medical, emotional, and/or physical challenges. It could also be the results of trauma, which is a difficult, disturbing experience with deep, long-lasting emotional, mental, medical, or physical consequences. A few types of trauma could include abuse, neglect, displacement, bullying, medical, injury, disaster, or death.

There is a difference between lacking family values and being temporarily unable to fulfill family responsibilities, and it is important that such circumstances not be misinterpreted or conflated.

When people desire and strive for the same goals, it brings cohesiveness. This can be seen when adult children pattern their own family traditions, careers, vacations—and even a desire for education—after what they saw as children within their family or tribe. Children who grow up in a home based on positive family values have a greater potential for staying focused, generating learning opportunities, and being prepared for life.

CHAPTER 4

Values Taught by the Tribe

A hundred years from now it will not matter what my
bank account was, the sort of house I lived in, or the
kind of car I drove … but the world may be different,
because I was important in the life of a child.
—Anonymous

I often refer to my tribe, which includes my core family members
(Mom, Dad, and my siblings), my extended family (grandparents,
aunts, uncles, and cousins), and close family friends, girlfriends,
neighbors, and church members. School staff and community
members are also in my tribe. There was always someone in my
tribe on whom I depended to teach me, lead me, assist me, and
hold me accountable for my actions and decisions. I would do the
same for them. They helped nurture family values and generate
learning opportunities. Some members of a tribe can fluctuate,
depending on the reason or season, whereas others are there for
life.

Values Taught by Extended Family

I remember traveling south to Tennessee and Alabama every summer for our Fourth of July weekend family reunions. It was a hot, long, and exhausting drive in a crowded car, but we had so much fun. The deep, hearty laughter could be heard throughout the vehicle. Sometimes I didn't even know why we were laughing, but that didn't matter. I simply joined in the fun. Even on our tight budget, each kid always had a brand-new pair of white tennis shoes and a new outfit to wear on the trip.

Our extended family was economically diverse. Although some had an abundance of resources to meet their family's financial and educational needs, others created prosperity from their more limited resources. They resided in Alabama and Tennessee, by way of Ohio and Michigan. When we were together, every gesture and movement displayed concern, appreciation, love, and respect. Conversations were courteous, polite, and respectful. The first sign of a disagreement, which happened infrequently, was quickly followed by smiles, forgiveness, hugs, and a gentle pat on the back, uniting spirits from deep within.

Even when the cousins had an occasional difference of opinion, we were expected to disagree in a respectful manner. There were various priorities and opinions, but they were met with high regard. Even with the best intentions and efforts, we were an ordinary family, which sometimes brought challenges, so open communication was an important family value.

Family reunions were a place to demonstrate family values each year. Family and friends would all gather around a big, country table filled with all types of delicious food. It was there that our parents administered the family values test each summer. Were their children kind, polite, helpful, and respectful to each other, cousins, aunts, and uncles—but most of all, to Grandma and Grandpa? During these gatherings, the Watkins kids' parents would express these expectations:

- Be on your best behavior.
- Don't argue and fight.
- Look out for each other.
- Share with one another.
- Don't tell our family business.
- Boys protect girls.
- Don't talk back to adults.
- Do what you are told … quickly.
- Don't get in grown folks' business or conversations.
- Know when to speak up.
- Know when to shut up.

Sometimes we fell short of the "don't" expectations, but they were designed to teach us to demonstrate respect (for self, others, others' belongings), courtesy, honesty, sharing, and other family values. This list of expectations has been a guide to my own parenting and perhaps could be of benefit for other families today.

Our family valued this extra barrier of protection shared at family reunions and gatherings, as this was our accountability time. Throughout the year this was part of our motivation to stay focused on study habits, homework, behavior, extracurricular activities, and everything connected. Many families may share some of our same values, although having values does not automatically guarantee high academic achievement. But having them in place will not hurt the process—if anything, it will help.

Values Taught by Church

Church and Bible scriptures created my foundational values. My most valued knowledge and life instructions about who I am, what I believe, how to value others, proper conduct, and family matters came directly from the Bible. From this source, I discovered that I can be forgiven, and I have the option to start each day fresh and new. These godly principles have been a comforting source of strength, and they touch every area of my thoughts, actions, and life.

Sunday Best

Even when opinions, options, and laws change, I can stay true to my core. It is important for me to know and understand this source of my values, which I found in the people in my tribe who surrounded me every day. These values were also developed in my early childhood Sunday school lessons.

I often use these Bible verses as a guiding force in my life:

- "Do unto others as you would have them do unto you" (Luke 6:31)
- "Love your neighbor as thyself" (Matthew 22:39)
- "Start children off on the way they should go, and even when they are old they will not turn from it" (Proverbs 22:6)

List here some scriptures, quotations, or sayings that you can use as a guiding force for the family values and desires of your life.

_____

_____

_____

_____

_____

_____

Values Taught by Neighbors

In the friendly neighborhood where I grew up, there were no highly educated or wealthy people. Everyone had the same basic priorities—home, food, clothing, car, education, family vacations, and church on Sunday morning. Families worked long and hard, and they respected, protected, assisted, and cared about each other.

I often found myself in the homes and intimately involved in the lives of family members and friends who had a positive effect on how I determined what really mattered. I did chores for family members and neighbors, babysat and played with their kids, assisted in their kitchens, or just sat and observed how they lived.

On our street, Mrs. Fears and Mrs. Drake would give me chores to do in their home, which often included looking after their children. Mrs. Steps and Mrs. Hamilton also helped lay the foundation for many of my family values. They were my role models because they took the role of motherhood seriously. Those women took care of and respected their family members, and yet they still had time for me. I did not know then that they were teaching me about responsibility and how to be a valued community member.

Our neighbors relied on each other and showed genuine concern for each other's well-being. That was how I acquired a spirit of servanthood—helping others discover and explore options or establish family values.

Life and people were somewhat different when I was a child; in my experience, most family adult matters were hidden from children. Today I encounter an uncomfortable number of people who appear to have, in my opinion, questionable values and opinions about what should be said and done in the presence of children. A child should not be exposed to family financial problems, negative communication, trying to help solve family or parent relationship challenges, or put in harm's way or danger. The adults in my tribe protected children—no matter what.

In life, things may sometimes become challenging, but a child's world should be focused on fun, play, school, caring people and experiences. Children deserve time with caring adults, and they should be safe with their families and in their schools and communities.

PART 2

Academic Achievement

CHAPTER 5

Academic Achievement Begins in the Home

I was dealt the same hand you were,
and I decided to win with it.
—E. N. Joy

We have defined academic achievement as the level of education or knowledge successfully gained, as shown by scholastic testing, knowledge demonstration, or performance assessments. Today we live in a fast-paced, ever-changing, globally competitive world of science, technology, engineering, and mathematics—referred to as the STEM disciplines—that crosses over every career field. An abundance of opportunities exist to incorporate basic fun into learning that can enforce reading and writing, which is essential for students who wish to prepare for things yet to come in our complex world.

The methods of teaching and learning implemented in many schools today will be new for some parents, who must look for new and creative ways to support and advocate for their children. Plans for a child's education should begin at the moment of conception. However, it is never too late to engage in the academic success of your child. We will talk about ways to connect at home and school, which begins with positive, empowering words of encouragement.

Studies indicate that most high-achieving students are in homes where parents or other adult caregivers are engaged in the educational process and demonstrate the value of education. It is essential that the home be a positive learning environment. Learning begins with stories and active hands-on lessons each day, which establishes the framework for academic achievement. Take the time now to establish your family values for academic achievement.

Neither of my parents completed high school, yet they saw education as a viable pathway. This must have been challenging in view of their personal, educational, and economic limitations. According to the US Department of Agriculture, the average cost of raising a child is slightly over $200,500 (www.cnpp.usda.gov). Despite restricted family finances, my parents implemented many strategies and techniques to keep five rambunctious kids on track. They guided us through the education pathway with high goals and family values. In our family, success was not an option—it was a requirement. I was fearful of the consequences that might result from slacking off in school.

My family values transitioned from the kitchen table—daily lessons of love and family gatherings—to academic achievement behind a classroom desk. Teachers benefited from the family values that were taught in our home and carried into the learning environment, which—I hope—made our parents proud.

Elementary School

As I started second grade at Robinson Elementary School, things seemed to go pretty well. However, I remember hiding behind students in front of me to avoid being called on to read out loud. While writing this book, I happened upon my second-grade report card. Under the "Growth in written expression" box, on a scale of one to three, my teacher gave me a one and wrote, in neat cursive, "Needs to improve."

As I reflected on this report card as an adult, I came to understand my elementary school practice of holding my head down to avoid eye contact with the teacher. My antics didn't always prevent the teacher from asking, "Gloria, can you read the next paragraph to the class?" My heart would pound as I responded, full of insecurity.

Although I lacked confidence, my family values led me to reply to my teacher and give my best response. I don't remember that anyone was aware of this challenge, not even my mom. We all read books at home for Mom, so how could I tell her that I couldn't read at school? There was a missing link—a big disconnect that went unnoticed at school while Mom did her best to monitor my progress. Parents have to be involved with the education of their children, and when questions arise, they should quickly seek out resources from the family team, school, and community. All children must learn to read early and remain at the grade level appropriate to their age.

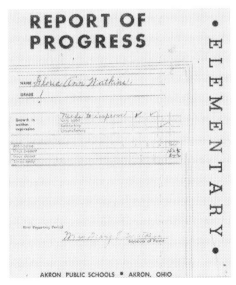

2nd Grade Glo   2nd grade "REPORT OF PROGRESS"

When I was in fourth grade, our family made the big move to West Akron. This was to my advantage, because my siblings and I were enrolled in higher-rated public schools. However, over a three-year period I attended three different elementary schools. Crouse was my fifth-grade school for one year until the school boundary changed, and then I was rerouted to Rankin for my sixth-grade education. I was not happy about yet another elementary school, because I had to make new friends all over again. For a young girl, friends were a major part of life.

The thing that I remember most about elementary school was finding myself in the middle of the English phonics debate. When I was in the fourth, fifth, and sixth grades, educators had differing views on the most effective method of teaching fundamental vocabulary. I have to believe that the educators in our school district did not intentionally make life difficult for their students, but I knew I was in trouble when my English teachers at three different schools had contradictory views on what should actually be taught. One teacher focused on teaching phonics, another claimed not to believe in phonics, and the third teacher didn't care one way or the other because most of her students were already proficient in English.

I was clever enough to eventually figure out how some parts of the English language functioned, but I never learned in a classroom how to properly sound out words. I developed my own coping skills below to get over the English hurdles:

- practicing known reading assignments ahead of time,
- talking with classmates about the reading assignments, and
- always having a phonics sheet or dictionary handy.

These strategies worked for me; however, I was not a candidate to win the spelling bee.

According to a study conducted by the Department of Education and the National Institute of Literacy, 32 million adults in the United States can't read. This is 14 percent of the population, including 19 percent of high school graduates who can't read. It is essential that parents and any tribe members read with small children daily. Not everyone in an academic situation similar to mine will have an opportunity to recover. I was fortunate to have a second chance, which made me work even harder.

Middle School

The English debate had a devastating effect on my academic achievement, because it slowed down my ability to master reading, literature, and language. There were no Reading Recovery classes or programs at that time, which meant that all children and their families had to face this challenge alone.

Today, within each school system there should be a literacy service to support the improvement of reading for *all* students. If necessary the English department or counseling office would be a good place to start your advocacy. My experience with English sparked my curiosity about school administration and legislation to benefit students and their families.

High School

My high school years were spent at Buchtel High School, home of the Griffins, where the great divide in social status became obvious. It was easy to determine not only which students were better off financially, but which students came from supportive or unsupportive families. Telltale signs included how students were groomed and dressed, whether they attended regularly and had lunch money, their relationship with teachers and school administrators, and their participation in extracurricular activities.

In the seventies there were two Home Economics academic tracks—one for those going to college, and another for those who were not. I had planned to attend a professional tailoring school in Philadelphia and live with my mom's sister, Aunt Ann, so I had not elected to enroll in college preparatory classes.

High School Graduation

During my senior year, I was intensely insulted and motivated by my home economics clothing instructor, Ms. Reese. One day she said to me, "Gloria, you can't go to college. You'd do better in a trade school." I suddenly recognized that she was not confident about my ability to succeed in college. Rather than discouraging me, her words filled me with a strong incentive to enroll, even knowing that I might not be adequately prepared academically or financially.

I had little knowledge of college requirements, cost, or the process for enrolling, but the assertiveness that my family valued, taught, and demonstrated was my motivation to learn and proceed toward the goal. College is not for everyone, but it is never too early to begin the conversation about educational pathways.

College Prep

My parents couldn't continue to provide for me financially after high school or contribute to my college expenses, because there were three children standing in line behind me. I worked hard to be able to pay my college expenses, including looking for scholarships and grants, although I tried to avoid loans as much as possible. As I did all this, I reflected on how my parents were the perfect examples of digging deep to meet obligations with respect and dignity. If I was ever to be self-sufficient, I would need to be assertive and take responsibility for my actions ... and my education.

While growing up, it never dawned on me that assisting with the care of my three younger siblings and babysitting the neighborhood children was training me to be dependable and responsible. Mom shared budgeting tips as I saved my babysitting money, which started me on the road to self-sufficiency.

My deep concern about the dysfunctional trauma experienced by my family—and other families like ours—generated my interest in family relations and human development (home economics), which later became my career choice. It was my responsibility to take what I had learned, my family values, and pursue an education that would prepare me to inspire positive family values, academic achievement, and personal success in others.

Mom was not familiar with the higher education process, but she offered her support. I don't remember Dad being involved in any education conversations, mainly because he worked the evening shift. I assertively sought guidance from school counselors, mentors, and community organizations. I had to do the hard work of exploring colleges alone, by attending information meetings and events.

I was advised to take both the ACT and the SAT, the standardized tests that are used to determine a student's preparation for college. For me, preparation for these tests required a lot of commitment, dedication, and practice. At eighteen years of age, I was more serious about education than ever before, as all of my familiar family values were staring me in the face.

College—Undergraduate

I first carried my family values to the School of Home Economics at the University of Akron. As a freshman, I took several remedial classes, which provided an opportunity to catch up with my colleagues. Then I was well on my way to graduation. I even surprised myself at what my respect, dependability, responsibility, self-sufficiency, assertiveness, and hard work ethic could accomplish. I chose affiliation with Delta Sigma Theta Sorority, an organization of college-educated women committed to public service. They became members of my tribe, support system and sisters.

After completing one and a half years at the University of Akron, I experienced an overwhelming desire to leave the comfort of my hometown—my family support, security, and friends—to venture out into the world. During my sophomore year, I decided to relocate to the big city of Columbus and continue my education. When I shared my desire with Mom, she said, "If you can figure it out, do it." As always, Mom was my biggest advocate. I transferred to The Ohio State University, which was an opportunity to take total responsibility for my own actions as I continued to work my way through college.

Moving expenses were difficult to manage but this gave me a chance to demonstrate self-sufficiency. I faced many of the normal college student challenges, including limited household budgeting experience. However, I had the advantage of excellent time management skills, and I was self-disciplined. I was not pressured by a distracting social life, however I did enjoy college. It was my family values that kept me grounded.

Many college students confront barriers. According to the National Center for Education Statistics, only 59 percent of first-time, full-time undergraduate students finish college. I made my family and tribe proud when I completed the requirements for my Bachelor's of Science Degree in Home Economics and graduated from The Ohio State in June 1974.

My parents divorced while I was in college as situations at home began to conflict with Mom's values and compromise the safety of our family. Mom was determined to raise my younger brother and sisters as a single parent, and she worked her way through this transition. She became employed full-time for the first time in her life, so that she could maintain her household and plan for our future.

Domestic conflict affects many families and has an astounding effect on the education of students. Changes in schools, living arrangements, and custody should be avoided during the school year whenever possible to avoid childhood trauma. Most children are resilient as long as they have family support, and children are better off in a loving, safe, secure environment.

Early Adulthood

Upon graduation from The Ohio State University, I immediately took a job in the conservative corporate business world—another case of unfamiliar territory. The uniform dress code included a suit in the basic colors of black, brown, blue, and gray, with a white or cream blouse. Jewelry was limited, and shoes were expected to perfectly match our clothes.

I recall the following saying: "You only have one chance to make a first impression." Fortunately for me, I had been somewhat exposed to business dress by watching my father get suited up to attend post office union meetings. He didn't have even a high school education, but he had learned valuable business protocols in his quest to be responsible, self-sufficient, and dependable for his family. Dad knew that clothes were important, because that's the first thing people notice about us. Whether accurate or not, opinions are formed based on what we're wearing.

Look for opportunities to involve children in age-appropriate, work-related conversations that can relate to academic and real-life scenarios. As I mentioned earlier, my mother was a stickler for making sure her children understood the importance of appearance—wearing clean, pressed clothing. Our clothes didn't have to be expensive name brands, but they had to be clean and look decent. Our family values for dressing with self-respect, together with responsibility, led us to make wise and acceptable clothing choices for work.

However, children can observe and imitate more from their parents than simply the importance of dressing appropriately. For example, I had not anticipated that marriage to my son's dad would end in divorce. However, I had observed the force to stay focused from Mom. That was a challenging, tough time for me, but I had to take the responsibility for reevaluating and reorganizing my life. Working full-time was the option I chose to support my son and myself. My work ethic would not allow me to think about anything except navigating through my situation. My loving, dependable tribe made it easier for me to balance life, work, and family, which for me included parenting, work, family, friends, and a social life outside of the home.

After my once-happy union split up, my primary goal was to avoid letting our situation interfere with the academic achievement of my rambunctious five-year-old son, Clifford. Not appearing to be traumatized by that life-changing event, he was eager to begin kindergarten and ride the "big school bus." I made the necessary changes to integrate all the activities that were important to Clifford. I volunteered at his elementary school and kept the lines of communication open with him, making certain that his homework was completed daily and that we both maintained high expectations.

These life experiences intensified my interest in family values and their role in academic achievement. I became more curious about why some families survive challenging times but others fall apart. I began to think that perhaps this topic needed further study ... by me.

Adulthood

Before completing my undergraduate program, it had been my desire to enter graduate school, because it was necessary for my chosen career pathway and would lead to my goal of working in academia. However, at that time, obtaining full-time employment was in my best interest. It was essential that I seek a work environment that would value my position as a single parent and allow for flexibility when necessary.

Ohio State's Young Scholars Program (YSP), a college preparatory program, provided an opportunity for me to work full-time while attending graduate school. This dream job allowed me to redirect the lives of families while advocating for academically promising, first-generation, potential college kids. I was making a difference in the lives of children from all over Ohio who were just like me. I had a chance to pay back and get paid while doing it. Not bad, huh?

That rewarding experience intensified my concern for the influence of family values on academic achievement among all students, but especially among minority families in financial need, similar to my own roots. The economic backgrounds and communities of YSP students mirrored those of my own childhood.

In 1994, I earned a master of liberal studies degree in humanities and human ecology. Fulfillment of my graduate degree requirements included a focus on the methods and practices successfully used by parents to transmit family values that influence academic achievement. Working with the YSP program, staff, students, and families was the ideal combination of work and education that allowed me to make a valuable contribution to generations of families.

Glo graduate school graduation - YES!

I value my deep community involvement and ability to stand on the firm foundation of family values that was laid by my parents. Along the way, I loved and trusted many supportive family members, friends, teachers, school administrators, mentors, church members, businesspeople, and community members. That was my educational journey, and I am thankful for the many educational and career opportunities along the way.

For those of you who want to pursue academic and career dreams, opportunity is available to you. It is best to start preparing children early in life with actions that support academic achievement. To help prepare your children for college, I suggest reading Norma J. Richards's book *Free Ride to College*, in which she shares how to groom your kids for a full academic scholarship. The same opportunities are available to every child, no matter their financial situation. Whether they dream of community college or Harvard, Norma shows that it can be a reality with the proper work, dedication, and educational family values.

"**Intelligence** plus **character**-that is the **goal** of true **education**."
—Martin Luther King, Jr.

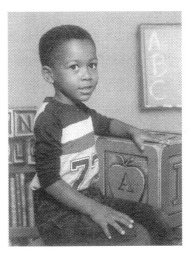

It's easy as ABC

CHAPTER 6

Duplicating the Next Generation

Vision without action is merely a dream. Action without vision
just passes the time. Vision with action can change the world.
—Joel A. Barker

My frustration level was high as I sat in an auto mechanic's shop
waiting to hear the cost of my car repair. I had just left work in
downtown Columbus, rushed to the far side of town to pick up
Clifford from school, and then backtracked to the repair shop for
services that could not be postponed. I sat there wondering where
I would obtain the money for the repairs. I reflected on Mom,
who took on financial responsibility without one complaint while
raising her three youngest children as a single parent. I wanted to
be self-sufficient, and in this case, that meant humbling myself
and accepting a payment plan from a member of my tribe.

While he sat in the shop, Clifford quickly did his fourth-
grade homework. Then he began exploring the Universal Classic
Cars shop and asking questions of Mr. Adrian, the mechanic/
owner from the Virgin Islands. They were engaged in a manly
conversation about batting averages, what team numbers belong to

certain players, and which years the Steelers won the Super Bowl and by exactly how many points.

Mr. Adrian was a successful neighborhood mechanic who also valued education. He enrolled his children in the best schools in our area. It was natural and effortless for him to mentor my son as he continued to work his automobiles. He was a member of my tribe who reminded me of how the ladies in my Akron neighborhood taught me about family values.

Right before my eyes, I was watching community encouragement take place with my son in his neighborhood mechanic's shop. This type of mentoring experience for a young man can also happen in a barbershop, on a sports team, in a neighborhood community center, or just with a male role model spending high-quality time with the child. Such relationships can be enriching, motivating, educational, and life changing.

Continued conversations with Mr. Adrian about scholarship opportunities led me to the perfect academic fit. He convinced me to look into The Wellington School for Clifford. Today some of my fondest memories of secondary education include the encouragement, good times and support, from Denise Hickson, Chris Robbins and Dr. Peter and Kristi Johnston. What started out as a frustrated, responsible, single parent in an auto mechanic shop turned into a rewarding community connection. If my car hadn't needed repairs, my son might have been robbed of a priceless mentoring moment and educational opportunity. Such stories increased my faith and reliance on family values, and assured me that God was behind the wheel and working on my behalf.

Many men shared in supporting, mentoring, coaching, and disciplining Clifford, including his dad, Leslie Cannon Sr., Dr. Dan Wilson Sr., Attorney Hanson Guest, Tim Eiler; pastors Keith Troy, Keith Bradley, David Forbes, and Charles Montgomery;

Jeff Fluellen, Larry Moore Sr., Vince Harris, David Cornute, Ernie Thornton and Joe Hamilton. My belief is that parents should offer suggestions and encourage their children to recognize potential mentors. Lead your children in identifying people who can lend a listening ear, spend time with them, and offer wise counsel. These connections can prove valuable and minimize the chances of making erroneous decisions.

All children are wired differently, which means they may require a variety of learning techniques. Parents should find a school that is a good fit for their child. Teachers, counselors, school administrators, and your local board of education can be valuable resources. When you find limited school options, connect with the school to identify the teacher who is the best fit for your child's personality and learning style.

Nearly all research says that students in a single-parent home are less likely to complete high school, and even less likely to earn a college degree. However, Clifford Cannon successfully earned a bachelor's degree in Business Information Systems, and a master's degree in Information System Management. Yes! I am the proud mama, and I am thankful to Clifford that he did not allow me to become a single-parent statistic.

Watching my son over the years has been interesting, because I have observed his family values both flourish and sometimes become challenged. We decided together that education would be important no matter what, and it has been a priority.

I sometimes talk with parents who had excellent family values, yet their children went astray. We must then meet our children where they are, focus on their strengths, stay connected, keep communication open (even if it is one-sided), love them, be patient, and wait until the storm passes. Remember, children should not be expected to be faultless, or else they would have no need for parents.

Clifford M. Cannon
Thank you my son for Generating Learning Opportunities

It Started at Home: Education Reflections

Being raised with strong family values and a sense of determination and deep love was lifesaving for me. My family had the same flaws with which many adults and children struggle still today, but I made a choice to not allow the undesirable situation to overpower my future potential. I was inspired to develop a positive attitude, display self-confidence, establish a vision, and set goals, because my parents constantly encouraged education and remained focused on personal and educational triumph.

On the other hand, it disturbs me greatly to witness or hear about innocent children who miss out on high-quality educational opportunities. Parents, families, and communities must advocate; share skills, time, and resources; and work together to fill in the gaps.

Strategies to Improve Academic Achievement

Every family that I have ever encountered, no matter how negative things may appear, has some measure of deeply ingrained, positive values—and those values must be our focus. It is important to recognize that children learn differently. Education begins in the home, and educators must study the differences among children and their cultures. A multicultural perspective on education will include understanding the values in the home environment. During the early formative years that shape their family values, young men are most at-risk in our educational system.

Classroom teachers, education administrators, and the entire school staff must get to know families by asking questions, and should attend school and community events outside the classroom. They should also inquire about the challenges that families face, which can be barriers to academic achievement, ask deeper questions, and help bridge the gap as student advocates.

Implications

Educators who do not enter the arena with similar family values or interest in gaining information bring yet another concern. Unfamiliarity with student family dynamics most directly affects educational goals and aspirations of children who have already experienced academic challenges. A restructuring of the educational system could include a curriculum that would emphasize an improved collaboration between students, families, schools, and their community.

PART 3

Actions That Support
Academic Achievement

Actions That Support Academic Achievement

Love

Open communication

High expectations

Parent involvement

Daily homework

CHAPTER 7

Love

Do everything in love.
—1 Corinthians 16:14, New International Version

Academic achievement has been a growing topic of discussion in communities worldwide. Today we see diversity and inclusion through a much broader lens, and various academic supports can be made available for all children. Many people share concerns about the low priority placed on commitment to academic excellence among some children. Along with many other experts and authorities on academic achievement, I am convinced that *action* in the educational process is the factor most necessary for change. Together, words and actions can make academics powerful. Identifying even the most common actions in the home provides insight into which family values are most influential when it comes to academic achievement and how they are translated into daily behaviors.

Parent, family, and community tribe members can benefit from added skills and competencies to help them enhance a child's learning; engage more deeply in the rigors of the education system; recognize and respond to potential education advantages and challenges; assist children in developing knowledge, skills, and relationships required to thrive in adulthood; and identify support and resources.

We have laid a foundation of family values with the building blocks of respect, dependability, responsibility, self-sufficiency, assertiveness, and a strong work ethic. I have offered explanations, definitions, and examples of how these values were woven into my family team by Mom, Dad, and my tribe—extended family, church members, and neighbors. When love, communication, high expectations, parental involvement, and daily homework are incorporated into the home, they aid in driving academic achievement.

Loving a child begins with love of self. It is important to respect and want the best for the person you see in the mirror, because only then will you have love to share with others. Unloving and unloved people are often lacking in confidence, fearful, and prone to anxiety. But with the right support, they, too, can reach any goal.

We can all be examples for a child who crosses our path. All people, including children, perform much better when there is someone walking along the sidelines offering support, encouragement, advice, and even sometimes discipline. Love means accepting your child for who they are, leading them in a positive manner, providing for them, and protecting them along life's journey.

Love **ACTIONS**
That Lead to Academic Achievement

Children of any age appreciate the many ways in which parents and others show they care. Imagine how a child would feel if they knew that you went out of your way to do something just for them. These simple gestures can help motivate and encourage students.

- Hide a handwritten note of affirmations, pictures, or letters to express your love in the child's pocket, book bag, or lunch box.
- On occasion, stop all activity and enter the child's world. Talk with them and attentively listen to what they have to say. (The importance of communication with children became a reality for me many years ago when, with a sad face, my son uttered the hurtful words, "Mommy, you are not listening to me." I quickly gave him my apology and full attention.)
- Spend time doing things they consider fun without distractions, and watch them really enjoy the special attention.
- Support your child by getting to know their teacher, attending school meetings, and being an involved parent.
- Prepare their favorite foods or visit the restaurant of their choice.
- Pray with and for your child.

Love Words That Lead to Academic Achievement (and Success in General)

Express words of love on a daily basis. They may seem small, but such words are a powerful and effective way to show that you care about a child and their future. Make these words echo in your child's ear:

- I love you.
- I'm proud of you.
- You're doing fine.
- I believe in you.
- How can I pray for you?
- I'm never too busy for you.
- You are the best!
- You are awesome!
- You are wonderful!

Now use this space to develop your own loving words:

_____

_____

_____

_____

_____

Whether you are a parent, guardian, family member, or valued member of someone's tribe, a child somewhere is depending on your love. Every child is different, with their own unique mix of likes and dislikes, but everyone can learn how to nurture. In *Parenting Your Children into Adulthood*, Dr. Ron Hitchcock offers tested and proven perspectives on how to form successful lifelong relationships with your adult children.

CHAPTER 8

Open Communication

Words mean more than what is set down on paper. It takes the human voice to infuse them with shades of deeper meaning.
—Maya Angelou, *I Know Why the Caged Bird Sings*

Communication can be loosely defined as simply a flow of information, usually between two or more people, with the goal of sharing a message. It can include both verbal and nonverbal actions such as spoken words or body language. This early childhood education learning skill makes it easier to interact, understand people in our world, and get needs addressed.

Open communication occurs when both the sender and receiver of the message are able to express their feelings, ideas, opinions, and concerns. In contrast, *closed* communication resembles a lecture in which one voice or point of view prevails. The most effective communication is when all parties feel that they are being heard equally without being evaluated or attacked. At the conclusion of the communication, there should be a sense of progress without regret. Parents with children of all ages should welcome and enjoy the opportunity to speak with their children without stress, conflict, or rebellion. This would make life more productive and enjoyable for the entire household, allowing more time for other tasks and fun family time.

All children deserve and benefit from having a responsible person with whom they can talk about anything, although it's best if that person is a parent. I say this because children will find someone to talk to, even if that person might not be the best choice for promoting a positive, successful life outcome. Invite responsible people to share words of affirmation and motivating conversations with your child. It is also helpful to surround them with positive role models who can provide a listening ear and speak words of inspiration.

All communication should be open and nonjudgmental, and the adult participants should strive to develop the best relationship possible with the child. Communicating is like playing pitch and catch—one minute you are delivering (throwing) a message, and the next minute you are receiving (catching) a message in return. The results depend on how well both players can catch and throw. Children are just learning how to catch and throw new information, which means that to be a winner, they will need your coaching at home, with friends, and at school.

Open Communication **ACTIONS**
That Lead to Academic Achievement

- Generate effective communication skills.
- Understand and follow communication protocol: rules, codes of conduct, systems, etiquette, or procedures.
- Set clear ground rules for chats, meetings, group decisions, and so on.
- Make messages simple; children can catch only a little at a time.
- Be polite; say *please, thank you, pardon me,* and *excuse me.*

- Determine the best timing to get your desired result.
- When you know the facts, just say it and don't ask questions. Otherwise you can put kids in a position to be dishonest.
- Speak with respect, because you have to be a good role model.
- Ask open-ended questions about school. (See examples below.)

Please do not ask students, "How was school today?" Ninety-nine percent of the time they will answer, "Fine" or "Okay," which does not provide the in-depth information needed to support learning. To obtain a more useful response, try these open-ended questions:

- What was the best [worst] part of your school day?
- Did any teachers call on you in class today?
- Which classes did you feel the best prepared for today?
- What was your favorite food at lunch?
- What subject did you have the most trouble with today?
- Did you see anyone sad or upset at school today?
- Did you feel sad [happy] at any time today?
- Did you feel comfortable in the clothing you wore to school?
- Would you like me to visit your school for any reason?
- If you could change one thing about your day, what would that be?
- What homework do you have tonight? Do you understand it?

Use the space below to list some questions of your own to ask a child about their school day:

_____

_____

_____

Effective Communication Begins with Listening

A major part of communication is listening. The sender produces a sound, and the receiver makes an effort to pay attention and take notice of what the speaker said. This interaction requires the speaker to

- know the facts,
- listen first and talk second,
- ask questions when unclear,
- not interrupt the speaker, and
- put their emotions on hold.

Here are responding techniques that can be used to more effectively reply with a positive approach.

Reflective listening: This technique is used to demonstrate understanding through nonverbal signs: (1) making eye contact and nodding; (2) verbally repeating what you heard, such as "I heard you say that the test was really hard"; and (3) confirming reflection, perhaps with an "Mm-hmm." Reflective listening demonstrates that you care and have a desire to understand.

I messages: Using this technique, you express how you feel about a certain situation by using the word *I* instead of *you*. When a child hears *you*, it can feel to them like you're casting blame and cause them to raise their defenses. For example, here's a positive I message: "I felt hurt when there were stops at other places before coming home after school as we agreed. I really value dependability and trust." The goal is to share how you have been affected by the child's actions and teach responsibility.

Exploring alternatives: This strategy involves exploring options for resolving problems or challenges by asking questions that begin with such words as *how*, *what*, *tell*, and *explain*. For example, "*How* did you miss the bus?" The goal is to encourage children to problem solve by exploring alternatives and options, which teaches self-discipline and self-sufficiency. When communicating with a child, try using the following skills for effective communication:

- Establish a gentle interactive environment, which will make conversations comfortable and inviting.
- Take a proactive approach and encourage talking about topics that could affect academic achievement.
- Don't speak from across the room, but have good eye contact and listen attentively.
- Continue to practice these skills, because just like with any game, practice makes perfect.

Have conversations about real-life situations. When he was still quite young, I developed the habit of sharing some of my daily experiences with Clifford, in the hope that he would share his day with me as well. We began having kid-friendly conversations about friends, school, work, play, and personal achievements, and those conversations continued throughout his childhood and into his young adult life. I always wanted to be the first person who came to mind when he wanted to share thoughts, ideas, visions, goals, and aspirations.

I enjoy talking to most young people, and I like the fact that they are often nonjudgmental, honest, and direct in their opinions. However, they sometimes need adults to help them filter conversations. In doing so, it's important to be open, honest, and trustworthy.

Ask children their views on current actual situations. Show them how you use your education or job skills for everyday matters. Point out the connection between school, work, and life. Talk about the weather, travel, and family. Take advantage of car rides and dinner table conversations. I involved my son in my work by opening conversations with questions such as these:

- Guess what happened today? I forgot to take my lunch.
- What would you do if your boss didn't treat you fairly?
- I applied for a job and was the best candidate, but someone else was selected. How do you think I should handle that?
- I requested a day off work but was denied. What do you think I should do?

Use words to encourage and praise children often. In the home, establish a calm, interactive environment to make learning fun and offer encouragement. Being overly controlling and harsh turns children off and limits their desire to learn. Just one word or phrase can be powerful and make an enormous difference, because a child responds better to a gentle, caring voice. Try to catch them off-guard with some of these positive words, and don't hesitate to try new ways of expressing your encouragement.

- Great job!
- Good work!
- I can tell you worked hard.
- You did a lot of work today.
- How did you figure that out?
- You've really improved.
- You'll get it. Keep on trying!
- No matter what, I will still be proud of you.
- Where did you learn to do that?
- Wow, that's cool!
- Great!
- I like that!
- Super!
- I can't wait to see you perform in your concert [game, play, etc.].
- Everyone makes mistakes. I know you'll learn important things from this.
- Wow—you make it look easy!
- I knew you could do it!

CHAPTER 9

High Expectations

We need to internalize this idea of excellence. Not many
folks spend a lot of time trying to be excellent.
—President Barack Obama

Parents should know their children best, be aware of their abilities,
and feel confident that they are capable of performing to their
fullest potential. Parents should be the ones to initially set high
expectations for academic standards, even before their children
enter a formal education environment. There is a noticeable
difference between what parents of academically low- and high-
achieving students say and do on a daily basis. When the bar is
raised early in life, children tend to uphold those same standards
throughout their educational journey.

High Expectation **ACTIONS**
That Lead to Academic Achievement

Reject negative attitudes. Parents must present to their children a positive, encouraging attitude about attending school and getting an education. Children must see the educational experience as necessary for a successful life. Have confidence that your child can be a high-achieving student.

If you had an unfavorable school experience, don't allow your adverse attitude to reflect onto your children. Believe me, even though they may not say anything, children will closely observe any negative vibes. Their initial feelings and thoughts about education will set the groundwork from kindergarten through postsecondary education. It is well worth the effort to present an optimistic outlook on the future for all young people.

Expect the best. Encourage students to put forth their best and perform well in school. Express your support often by saying, "You can do or be anything you desire, and you'll be successful!" When we encourage children to do their best and set high expectations and standards, that will overflow into other areas of their lives—financial, social, personal development, career, physical, family, and spiritual.

Don't compare. It is not helpful to compare children with each other, because each child has their own unique creative design. The parents' job is to advocate for children according to their individual learning styles and capabilities.

Demonstrate that education is a priority. When parents develop good relationships with their children, they feel better about listening. They then become more open to communication about school in general, and conversations about high expectations come more easily. Demonstrate the value you place on education by making it a high priority.

Require school attendance. Make it crystal clear from the beginning that you expect your child to attend school—on time, all day, every day. In our high-tech culture, sitting in a classroom can be seen as a waste of time. It's true that some of the most enriching education experiences take place outside of the classroom, and occasionally things happen that require a child to be absent. Nonetheless, school attendance is important.

Expect rigor. Expect your child to earn above-average grades, and watch for additional indications of a desire for excellence based on the child's ability level. Help students establish short-, mid-, and long-term academic goals. Students often will put forth more effort when expectations are clear. Notice their progress, and applaud their achievements.

Minimize distractions. Assist your child's efforts to stay focused by helping them

- set priorities of important tasks and activities,
- write down schedules and review them regularly,
- notice signs of negative peer pressure, and
- avoid things and people that are not supportive of their goals.

Develop leadership. For some children, leadership skills are natural, but they can also be learned. Parents who expect leadership from their children will reap the benefits all along the education and career journey. Try these ways to nurture this valuable quality:

- Start early to teach responsibility in the home.
- Create opportunities to make decisions.
- Send your child to summer camps that offer great opportunities to learn teamwork (and later to demonstrate their abilities as counselors).
- Encourage your child to engage in group work teams, which can impart proper business protocols and procedures.

Assist teachers with setting high expectations. The expectations a teacher brings into the classroom for each and every child are vitally significant for student achievement. It is common for characteristics such as race, ethnicity, gender, household income, and/or family status to influence our initial opinions of other people. The initial student/teacher relationship will shape not only expectations for academic achievement, but also the student's feelings of acceptance, encouragement, and overall support.

Meet with teachers to discuss your student's classes, homework, and overall education challenges. Ask what you can do to enhance the educational experience.

Likewise, teachers who view students negatively are less willing to offer encouragement or connect with their family. My first big parent advocacy experience occurred when my son was in kindergarten. I had decided that rather than purchase a bunch of toys for Christmas, we would take a trip to visit my brother in Hawaii. This was a wonderful family educational experience—we made a budget, tracked our trip on a map, checked the weather, and read books about our destination leading up to the trip.

Upon returning to school, Clifford was excited to share his experience with his classmates and teacher. After school, I noticed that he had a very sad face, and as we began to chat, he shared with me that his teacher didn't believe that he had gone to Hawaii. You know that Mama was at school the next day to inquire about that teacher's disbelief. Her words were "Well, you know how children sometimes stretch the truth." I firmly explained that we *had* taken a trip to Hawaii over the winter break, but she just smiled and offered no apology. It was my responsibility to focus on our fun time, assure Clifford of my trust and belief in his word, and help him to understand that people can be challenging sometimes.

The parents' role as advocate is to help the teacher and other school administrators see their child's potential for adding value to the world, which is well worth the time spent working toward high academic achievement. A successful, engaging, positive parent-teacher partnership works in the best interest of families and educators, because it provides an opportunity for all concerned to talk and develop a plan of action.

Know what affects classroom grades, promotions, and graduation. Every assignment, test, and grade is important. Identify the requirements early, and begin to prepare your child to meet them. High levels of success are achieved when the educational environment has structure and the child can focus on their high expectations. It is counterproductive when the goal is just to move students on to the next grade level. Not everyone is an A student, but the desire to learn can last a lifetime.

Explore career options. Provide opportunities for your child to explore interests outside of school, but don't be surprised when their choices are connected to their personal value system. To learn some of your child's interests, try asking the following questions:

- What do you like to do?
- What are your skills? What do you do best?
- What would your friends say about your interest?
- What gets you really excited?
- What do you like to do with free time?
- What are your favorite subjects in school?
- What do you see yourself doing as a profession?

Embrace ahas! When you see that spark of interest in your child's eyes, put things in action by exploring age-appropriate learning activities. For example, if you notice that your child has an interest in helping people, they might enjoy reading books or magazines about helping others. They may also like

- helping a younger child at school;
- assisting with hands-on community service projects;
- volunteering at a hospital;
- serving as a student member on a committee or board; or
- identifying their own mentor.

Children's interests change often, and early years are the best and least expensive time to explore. There are a lot of interest inventories on the Internet, and a school guidance counselor might be a good person to help identify your child's desires, review the results, and map out a career pathway. Students who discuss career interests with their parents and visit worksites together are more likely to pursue those interests after high school.

Expect lifelong learning. Parents have an opportunity to develop a yearning in their child for knowledge by simply making learning and education fun. Don't talk only about graduation from high school, but expect learning to continue beyond. Options could include a postsecondary degree from a graduate or professional school, career technical education training or certification, traveling the world with the military, or becoming a homemaker. Most occupations will require some form of postsecondary education. Read books together, search the Web together, and make vacations educational and fun. Conversations you have about life after high school will inspire exciting dreams, goals, and aspirations, and have the capacity to remove all boundaries.

It is important for students to connect the long-term benefit of today's building blocks to academic success. Parents or tribe members can help them realize that earning potential, lifestyle, jobs, and future goals are all based on academic outcomes. Whether students choose to work in the corporate or nonprofit world, travel the world or stay home and raise a family, some level of education is necessary.

CHAPTER 10

Parent Involvement

Not every teacher is a parent, but every parent is a
teacher. The most important thing a parent can give a
child is the sense of the importance of education.
—William Bennett, US Secretary of Education, 1985–88

It is absolutely essential that parents play an active role in the
education of their child at home and school. Parents come in all
shapes and sizes, and they have various kinds of relationships with
their children. Parenting can be done by a variety of adult authority
figures—birth parents, adopted parents, family members, or
court-ordered caregivers. Decades of research prove that student
academic achievement improves when parents take a leading role
in their children's education. Students need to know that someone
cares about them, which motivates their interest in learning and
makes them more likely to display positive behavior and social
interactions.

Students who do well academically are better prepared for
the demands of higher education and the technology-focused
workforce, which provides them with more life options. They
are more likely to excel in careers that lead to higher earning

potential. Students who do well academically also tend to have higher self-esteem, and they're less likely to use illegal drugs and other harmful substances.

Studies indicate that most high-achieving students come from homes where their parents are advocates and involved in the educational process. Parents are the first line of defense for assuring that their children have access to high-quality education that will meet their individual needs. Different types of schools—public, private, charter, magnet, community, special needs, career technical, military, boarding, and at-home—offer different benefits to fit a family's unique requirements and the student's specific needs.

Parents must accept a leadership role in monitoring the physical, mental, and social aspects of their child's growth and development, because they will want to be the first to offer praise or take corrective action. Much of a child's waking day is spent at school, so teachers see the child in the classroom and at play, and they know how their students interact with adults and other children.

Educators, family members, physicians, friends, and the entire community tribe can take a support role in the education process. They can serve as mentors, reading buddies, coaches, classroom monitors, homework helpers, tutors, or adult friends for the child. Regardless of their specific role, they can all make helpful observations, and they're all valuable members of the family team.

Involvement in education can be more fun with the support of others. Let's explore a few ways to take action in supporting a child's academic achievement.

Parent Involvement **ACTIONS**
That Lead to Academic Achievement

Try to see your child as a seed that came in a packet without a label. Your job is to provide the right environment and nutrients and to pull the weeds. You can't decide what kind of flower you'll get or in which season it will bloom.

—Anonymous

<u>Parent Involvement at Home</u>

Your home is a classroom. Generate learning opportunities in your home by incorporating a variety of real-life teaching principles into your daily routine. The opportunity to engage children in the home by teaching life skills to them is often neglected. Take advantage of occasions and create activities to teach your children and develop their skills, from the youngest child to the teenager. Here are suggestions to generate learning opportunities in your home every day:

SKILL DEVELOPMENT	ACTIVITY
Learn to follow directions	Fold clothes and napkins, dust furniture, and put items away in drawers. Locate items in a right or left drawer, top shelf, etc.
Learn to listen	Observe an alarm clock, doorbell, stove timer, phone ringing, or animal sounds. Repeat a statement to you.
Learn colors	Compare colors of fruits, vegetables, and clothing.

Learn shapes	Compare shapes of fruits and vegetables (banana, grapes, celery, pineapple), book sizes, and furniture.
Learn to organize	Sort clothes, make grocery lists, recycle, and plan a meal.
Learn flavors	Compare tastes of chocolate ice cream, bananas, oranges, grapes, and fruit punch.
Learn time management	Set times for meals, play, bed, cooking different recipes, and curfew.
Learn to read	Practice reading cereal boxes, canned-food labels, cooking directions, schoolbooks, newspapers, billboards, and street signs. Start a family book club.
Learn to write	Practice writing family names, addresses on greeting cards, grocery lists, and to-do lists. Set aside time for journaling.
Learn science	Ask questions about where faucet water comes from, what makes water boil, where dust comes from, what makes light switches work, and how the refrigerator stays cold.
Learn technology	Use computers, tablets, and smartphones to gather information and play games.
Learn math	Count items such as measuring cups, silverware, and dishes. Review newspaper ads for best prices, develop personal budgets, and analyze sports team data.
Your ideas here	

Recognize and embrace various learning styles. As I mentioned in an earlier chapter, every child is different. Children have a variety of learning styles and diverse methods of reaching their academic goals. Begin to identify how your child's brain is wired, so that you can determine the best way for them to learn. This can be the beginning of achieving their desired academic goals, because when you discover how they absorb information, you will know how to teach in the home—*and* you can share your findings with their teachers. Your child may use each of these learning styles at one time or another, which is perfectly acceptable and common.

Learning styles	Learn best with
Visual learners	Eyes—learn best when they see what they are learning and doing
Auditory learners	Ears—learn best through what they hear when learning
Kinesthetic learners	Body movement—learn best by actively doing something

To start determining how your child is wired and which style of learning may best suit them, say a word and ask them what comes to mind. Let's practice this concept with water. If they visualize a swimming pool, they might be visual. If they hear water splashing, they might be auditory. And if they feel the water against their skin, they could be a kinesthetic learner. To learn more, also observe them at school while playing. Ask their teacher, and don't forget to ask the child their personal preference.

There are also challenges to achieving academic success, and one common challenge is learning disabilities. If you suspect that your child has a learning disability, according to the Learning

Disabilities Association of America, your first step is to understand that when parents are involved in school, it is less likely that special education will be the first option for a challenged child. With the right support, every person can find success.

Having a supportive academic team of administrators and teachers can be a vital part of achievement. Parents can now access many tools and resources to become more informed advocates for their children. This information can be your foundation for actions that complement academic achievement, and it's never too early to begin. Please see some of the helpful resources listed at the end of this book.

Prepare for a fulfilling new school year. Organize your schedule and make health screening appointments, and identify school-supply requirements and appropriate uniforms or clothing. Rearrange your family schedule if necessary to ensure that your child gets eight hours of sleep every night. Have a regular homework time *and* time to relax. Set priorities, manage time wisely, establish a routine, and remember to spend one-on-one time with each child. Not every day will be perfect, and unexpected things will happen. But it is always helpful to be assertive and take responsibility for having a family plan.

Be informed. Read the school's mission statement, guidelines, and handbook, and be certain that your child adheres to appropriate school conduct requirements. Read the school newsletters and visit the school website frequently to remain updated on school changes, events, and activities. Also sign up for any email correspondence the school offers.

Early Learning Makes a Big Difference

Talk. As you move around the home, engage your children in conversation and encourage them to respond.

Read. Begin reading to your child early on. This can include books, grocery labels, and street signs, which will all increase their vocabulary. Reading is the foundation of knowledge, and it is unlikely that a poor reader will do well in other subjects. Begin to have your child read out loud to adults as the listener gives their full attention.

Write. As you write with your child, watch their motor skills improve.

Play. Research says that the value of play should not be underestimated. Play allows children to engage in the work around them, be creative, and make decisions—all of which aid in growth and brain development.

Inform the teacher. It is the parent's duty to make the teacher aware of any academic challenges they might notice with homework, testing, or other schoolwork. When children face a problem, immediately seek assistance at the school, but also ask teachers what can be done in the home to assist.

Use technology. This is an area where I find parents have to be good examples, since technology affects all ages. Smartphones, computers, tablets, video games, and the Internet keep us in touch with family, friends, and the world in general. They can also help keep parents in direct communication with their child's teacher. These devices are a source for education support and resources, because parents can now easily log in to the school's portal to see class assignments and school updates. Technology is here to stay, so the focus should be on how to make kids safe while using technology for educational purposes, and in fun and positive ways. Review your family values, and together establish rules for the digital age.

Entertainment. Television, music, and movies are part of our world—and very important to most children. However, their use should be monitored. Do these things together and discuss what you see or hear based on your family values. Playing games with the entire family is an opportunity for everyone to relax, spend high-quality time together, and just have fun. This will become a value and create lasting family traditions and memories. Parents and other adults can inconspicuously teach children leadership strategies and communication skills that they can later model in the classroom or other group settings. This can enhance your relationship with your child while making homework and test reviews more comfortable and stress-free.

Visit classrooms without walls. Provide interesting and fun active learning opportunities that will add to your child's knowledge base. For example, visit a library, art gallery, park, museum, zoo, historical site, farmers' market, musical or theatrical performance, or sporting event. Also encourage your child to participate in after-school clubs, classes, sports, and other extracurricular activities. These will ignite their curiosity in the environment and world.

Parent Involvement at School

Monitor school. In our busy world, it is sometimes challenging to daily check a child's educational status, but it is necessary to keep up with academics, especially when there may be difficulties. Parents should make it their business to be active at school, get to know the other adults, and share their desire to be involved in the education process.

Stay informed. Engage with the school through email and phone calls, or text on a consistent basis. Some parents use written notes in a daily or weekly student progress notebook. Many schools now have interactive websites where parents can access the school calendar, homework assignments, test dates, and grades.

Visit the school. A personal visit will help to develop a relationship with the teachers, principal, and staff. Share with them the academic, career, and social visions you have for your child.

Get acquainted. Parents should know not only the teachers and school administrators, but also the friends of their students and the friends' parents. Building this network helps you be connected and aware of things going on in the school environment. I am a big believer in parent power. Keep an open ear, and you might be surprised at what you learn.

Hold teachers accountable. Teachers should keep you informed of your child's actions, both positive and negative. Everyone is busy, but this is a team that must work together in the best interests of all children. Communicate with the teacher often, especially when your child is doing well, because it sends the message that you care about your child's education. Children also need to know that their efforts are noticed, valued, and appreciated, which encourages them to keep up the good work.

Attend school-related events. At the beginning of the school year, mark your calendar to attend parent-teacher conferences, Parent Teacher Association (PTA) or Parent Teacher Organization (PTO) meetings, fun nights, and sporting events. Also look for volunteer opportunities.

Be an advocate. Positively advocating for your child is a primary parenting responsibility. This includes defining and examining your concerns, developing potential solutions, meeting with the teacher to consider educational options, and following through with the educational plan. High student achievement is directly related to parent involvement with school.

CHAPTER 11

Daily Homework

Never put off the homework for tomorrow
that you can do today.
—Gloria "Glo" Redding

Homework is defined as an assignment or task given to students by a teacher that may include reading, writing, studying for a test, working on a project, or other responsibilities. For most students, homework is completed in the home. One major theme of a high-performing student is "homework every day," because homework helps students reach full academic achievement.

I have never encountered a successful student who did not do regular academic work outside the classroom. Homework should be designed as a way to review newly acquired knowledge, learn additional information and skills, and build a foundation for more difficult learning. It should help prepare students for increasingly difficult tasks and higher-order concepts. When students are not required to do homework, they see it as unimportant and they're not motivated to do the work necessary to excel. They tend to rely on short-term memory, they don't attempt to learn on their own, and they're unable to recognize the value of hard work and responsibility.

African American students sometimes have a unique set of environmental barriers, family relationships, economic, health, social, emotional, security, and other issues that affect their academic and personal development. This is not meant to suggest that other minority groups do not face their own unique obstacles, but simply shared from my own personal experiences. Families must cope with all such factors in the home while still preparing their children for school, which can result in getting their homework completed late. However, what begins as a homework routine in childhood can grow into excellent study, time management, personal development, and work skills in adulthood.

Daily Homework **ACTIONS**
That Support Academic Achievement

Because it is designed to take place in the home, homework is an area where parents can take an active role in the success of their children. They must be actively engaged in planning and implementing effective rules, structure, and strategies. The suggested ways to do so listed below can act as a guide.

Homework tasks should be done at home every day as a review of the current day's class work, preparation for the next day, studying for a test, and working on team assignments, special projects, or other work at home. Establishing a daily routine for homework is of utmost importance. Although sometimes homework can be stressful, it should be a priority, but it should not interfere with bedtime. Balance homework with giving the family time for fun and relaxation, both individually and together.

Flexibility should be permitted based on the child's age, after-school responsibilities, and preferences, because we all have different internal clocks. Students could be permitted to do other things before homework. If they are tired from a long school day, perhaps a short nap would provide energy. Others may be hungry and want a snack, or even early dinner. Some may find it relaxing to watch television, listen to music, watch a video, talk on the phone, check email, or even spend time playing as a transition into homework. Parents are the experts on what is best for their children.

Where a student does their homework is important. In your home, identify the most suitable environment for homework. It should be a quiet space with adequate lighting, and away from distractions. Preferably, it should be a place that could be used daily. Provide a desk or workspace, but note that some students prefer to study or read in a more relaxed area with a sofa and a few pillows. Students should be prepared with school planners, assignments, and books, and the area should be stocked with paper, pencils, markers, and other necessary supplies. An unprepared student is often the sign of a disorganized, overwhelmed parent or an academic challenge, which must be addressed for full academic achievement.

I am often asked if **music or television** should be permitted in the background. Although ambient noise is not helpful to most students, this parenting decision should be based on the individual child and their task, academic history, and learning style—and in any case, the music or TV should be monitored. Answering phone calls, texts, emails, and so on should become secondary during designated studying time. At the right time, there is value in using music, television, and other electronics as an aid to learning, but the time should be selective and measurable.

Implement a daily routine for checking homework that encourages students to take responsibility for carefully checking their own homework. Establish disciplined study habits by setting a time to begin and end. Review the homework with your child to make sure it's complete and correct. If you are unsure about their understanding of the assignment, ask them to explain their answers. If you're still uncertain, depending on the child's age, check with the teacher or ask the child to seek assistance or tutoring. Many schools provide homework helpers or other ways for parents to electronically stay in contact. Take advantage of this tool. It is smart parenting to network with other parents to confirm school events and activities, and to share ideas, tools, and resources.

Together with your student, develop a **written, measurable academic plan** that includes current and expected classroom performance, grades, and a time frame for advancement and improvement. Regularly monitor your plan, and seek support if necessary.

Allow the student to have **increased responsibility**, but always keep an open ear. Help your child obtain information about upcoming tests by asking them questions and offering gentle reminders. For younger children, communicate with the teacher what you are implementing at home, and ask for other ways that you might help your child. Frequent discussions and updates can help identify problems early.

No homework? I occasionally hear parents say, "My child completes their homework and assignments at school." First, as a concerned parent, I would ask to see the completed product daily to make certain that it meets your family value expectations. Certainly, conference with the school to confirm that homework has been done in an acceptable and timely manner. Perhaps your expectations are different from those of the school, or perhaps your child is capable of doing more rigorous work. Can you imagine how your child might excel if they had additional academic challenges at home?

A very smart parent came up with the idea of creating homework when there were no homework assignments given by the teacher. Invite the child to choose a subject that interests them, and make it the topic of study. Reading or research during the scheduled homework time will creatively provide extra time for learning. Always celebrate each achievement.

PART 4

What Families and Students Say

CHAPTER 12

What Families Say

My personal, professional, community engagement, and volunteer experiences have embraced family focus interaction. For as long as I can remember, I have been curious about how family values influence academic achievement. I could tell you everything that I've experienced, read, studied, and researched, but you'll also benefit from hearing directly from other families who have experienced a similar journey.

Fulfillment of my graduate degree included a project with Ohio State's Young Scholars Program. These potential first-generation college students shared the challenge of needing financial assistance to attend college. I remembered so vividly when I was in their position. My major emphasis was on the methods successfully used by parents to transmit family values. I wanted to understand which everyday practices played a role in these students becoming academically successful.

The YSP parents and students were willing to share the effect of family values on the lives of their family and children at home and school. My goal was to gain additional perspective—not to judge the participants' family values or how they decided to lead their children to academic success. We provided questions simply to gain a deeper understanding of the connections between family values and academic achievement.

YSP students were expected to participate in all parts of the program leading up to twelfth grade. The components included academic enrichment, personal development, career exploration, cultural events, mentoring, parent alliance participation, and a summer academy. Upon graduation, they were eligible for assistance with the Ohio State application and scholarship process.

The next three chapters of this book are designed to share the common realizations and strategies offered by the participants. I believe in learning from others, but please remember that every child is different. YSP students and their families talked about their accomplishments, achievements, defeats, and success along the educational journey from their own family values perspectives.

YSP Program Project

For this project, adult and student family members of the YSP were randomly selected and asked open-ended questions. Those participating were high-achieving African American and Appalachian students between the ages of twelve and fifteen. Neither the adolescents nor the parents appeared to be affected by the presence of each other, and there was an obvious comfort level between the children and the adults. (Several grandmothers and older sibling caregivers were also chosen, as they were guardians at the time.)

This poll was not intended as a statistically sound instrument, and it might not be exact or error-free. However, I believe that the participants responded genuinely and honestly, sharing their family values and their academic and personal experiences. Perhaps they benefited from an opportunity to reflect on areas of success and need for improvement. As you read their comments, consider joining them by conducting your own family values and academic achievement self-assessment, using these same questions.

CHAPTER 13

What Parents Say

Parent Questions and Answers / GLO Comments

1) What family values account for the successful educational performance of your child?

Parent A: "For us, education has been a family value that has been passed down. My mom, who didn't have a college education, still valued and believed that education was important. In order to get the things you want in life, you need the education. As a parent, it's the best thing that I can do for my son. I kind of leave his career decisions up to him, but whatever that future is, it will start with an education."

GLO comment: Identify and begin teaching values early in life, because it can set the foundation for a more successful academic experience. When family values are clear and firm, students make more informed career choices because they respect the wise advice of others. Education requires responsibility, is very important, and will provide advantages in both the personal and professional life. It can lead to better jobs, independence, and self-sufficiency.

Parent B: "I basically started family value training with my children at birth. In order to receive, you have to give. But there are also rules to follow, like being home. She has a certain time to be home, and she must go to church on Sunday morning."

GLO comment: Establishing values early is always more beneficial than trying to undo or change certain values later. Children who learn to respect their parents will have fewer problems respecting their teachers at school, because they will know what respect looks like.

Parent C: "Education is needed for anything you do in life. I value education with my children and keep on track of their work assignments. It is important, because teachers could lose their grades and we will then have proof. I have them study more when they get a bad grade. I remind them and show them that education is important. I'm thirty-four and finally getting back to school for my undergraduate degree. This shows them that it is never too late."

GLO comment: Parents should have some idea of homework assignments and when they are assigned. This information can be obtained from the student, teacher, and sometimes online. Another option might be to talk with a classmate's family.

Interest in education doesn't have to stop at a certain age. Students should aspire toward lifelong learning. Setting an example is one of the best ways of displaying the high value you place on education. Students can see firsthand the commitment and time required to be high achieving. Actions can take the place of many words.

2) What do you do to encourage the educational success of your child?

Parent A: "We are involved in all activities; I want her to do well in school. That is the main thing that I believe in. We address the small problems before they become big, and teachers have the phone number where they can call if there is a problem. We don't want to wait until grades come out to know that she has failed and then start calling. If friends are not doing the same thing that you are doing, then drop them. We try to instill these values in her, but it is hard because she is a teenager."

GLO comment: When parents work outside the home, school involvement can be more challenging. However, it is always essential to stay involved and maintain close contact with teachers before problems arise. If necessary, involve your support team to make school visits and monitor activity, or identify other ways to be in the academic presence of your child.

Friendships are an important part of a teen's world, and establishing family values early in life will help provide guidance in selecting and maintaining friendships throughout life. It is easier to monitor a preteen's association with friends, because the child cannot yet drive and the parents have more control.

It's often difficult to drop friends, simply because being without friends is lonely. Encourage students to join school activities and go places where they can make new friends who share their values. When I was faced with this challenge as a teen, an older mentor shared with me that "if your friends see that you are not engaged and excited about their activities, they will often drop you first." However, it is a good idea to always be that little fly hovering over your child.

Parent B: "I expect my child to always be above average in academics and in her value choices, especially in today's society."

GLO comment: Parents should encourage their children to do their best, which includes making good value choices. Young people today are faced with many options and need the support and guidance of responsible adults.

Parent C: "At home, I encourage her because she is a born leader and wants to be an attorney. If that is what she intends to pursue, she will definitely be successful. I see her as a leader and someone who will put back into her community."

GLO comment: Students who are motivated and involved in their community do perform above average academically, because they gain more purpose from life. Not all children possess that internal excitement about school. Motivation is something that happens over time, building momentum after each conversation, success, act of love, and word of praise. It is important to find out what excites your child and use it for what I call "parent leverage." Provide increasingly challenging, interesting, responsible opportunities to learn and grow at school and home. This may be a good place to perhaps call on a tribe member to assist.

3) How do you help your child stay focused on school?

Parent A: "I listen."

GLO comment: Take time and make a conscious effort to stop and listen—to hear what your child has to say. If that is temporarily impossible, give them a specific time and location so that they can look forward to continuing the conversation later. Open communication is a major component of academic achievement. Parents talk a great deal to their children, but listening is equally important. I recall on several occasions my young son trying to get my attention when I was busy. I will never forget the look in his eye as he realized that I wasn't listening. I don't remember what I was doing at the time, but I will always remember his sad face.

Parent B: "I work, and when I get home, he will be studying. If he has a problem or any questions, we sit down and talk about how to solve the problem."

GLO comment: Parents are busy people, but it's important to find time each day to connect with your child about school, as a demonstration of your values around education. Positive, open communication is one way of saying to a child, "You are of value and important to me."

Parent C: "I help him to focus on both his long- and short-term goals. He is encouraged to study and keep his life together, to succeed in life, and to better himself. I want him to succeed in life. I don't want him to grow up like I grew up."

GLO comment: Parents who have experienced struggles have a lot to offer their children about how to avoid the pitfalls caused by unwise decisions. Goal setting can certainly keep a person focused. This can be done by writing down goals and regularly monitoring them for progress or as a sign for a need to change direction.

4) Why is it important for your child to succeed educationally?

Parent A: "I say to him, 'If you fail, then we all fail.' We know that he has the ability [to succeed]."

GLO comment: Students perform much better when the expectations are higher and others are depending on them to do well in life.

Parent B: "She stays right on top of her work. Most of the time, I leave it up to her. I check on her to make sure she has completed her homework, and I keep posted on her test scores. She is really self-dependent. I know that she can do the work and it is important to reach for the top."

GLO comment: Some students are independent, but they still often evaluate their family values to make sure that expectations and goals are clear. Parents should involve older students in identifying programs, resources, and other assets to enhance their education. It will take support, guidance, and resources to work through the maze of academics and career choices.

Parent C: "I tell her all the time that she has the ability [to be] successful, and I encourage her. She has no choice but to take education seriously if she wants the better things out of life, and it is also important to give back to your community."

GLO comment: Parents and primary caregivers are the people in a child's life who should stay positive, optimistic, confident, and hopeful in all situations. If necessary, invite your tribe in for support, because success is achieved best with a team effort.

GLO Comments to Families

Education is like a foundation for building life outcomes that will serve you forever. Good education practices and principles should be established at the beginning and progress gradually based on the age, learning style, and abilities of the child. It pays off, especially when you realize the employment wage difference between high school– and college-educated employees, or technical education training and certified employees. College also provides the opportunity to gain diverse skills and knowledge. However, college is certainly not the only way to acquire diversified skills.

All parents interviewed played an active role in the education of their children at home and school. They made it their business to get to know the teachers and staff, and make them aware of their desire to be involved in their child's educational process. This means the teachers get better acquainted with the students, who cannot get away with much nonproductive behavior. Also, parents are positioned to be well-informed advocates for their children should challenges arise, and they're the first to be informed of their child's success.

CHAPTER 14

What Students Say

Student Questions and Answers / GLO Comments

1) What family values account for your successful educational performance?

Student A: "Mom and Dad always stressed education in our family. There were ten of us, and we all had the chance to do better. They always stressed that they wanted us to do better in our life than what they did."

GLO comment: This reply echoes the words of my parents. Neither graduated from high school, but they had an encouraging desire for their children to reach higher goals. They did the hard work, made the sacrifices and laid down the family values. Mom stayed involved at school, monitored the homework of five children and also communicated with us openly and often. This demonstrated their love for us—even though as kids, we didn't necessarily call it love.

There were occasions when I questioned whether my son was hearing anything that came out of my mouth. I followed the academic achievement blueprint that my parents provided, and we still faced challenges. However, not once did we forget the value of education and our goals. Clifford completed his undergraduate degree and then announced that he was continuing school to earn his master's degree. Remember, this is my story, and all children are different. Get involved with your child, know their learning style and goals, what they like, and what other people see in them, and then help them map out a plan and go for it! Whatever *it* is, support them with high expectations.

Student B: "My parents teamed up on me and never allowed anything but my best. I learned fast and early that I was responsible for my school work."

GLO comment: This is a prime example of high expectations. Together, parents and teachers should establish goals based on the student's learning potential. Use benchmarks based on the very best schools, which—in our global economy—will be necessary to be competitive.

Student C: "I knew that my family was depending on me to do well as the oldest in my family. It felt good to get high grades, and I knew they were depending on me."

GLO comment: This sounds like the beginning of positive peer pressure among siblings, which can be powerful and fun. Students try harder when their academic potential is acknowledged. Remember—and I can't reiterate this enough—that every child will have their own interests, learning styles, and capabilities.

2) **What do you do in your home to demonstrate interest in academic achievement?**

Student A: "I come home and spend time doing homework, catching up on things, and working ahead."

GLO comment: It is important to have an after-school schedule to maintain focus and momentum.

Student B: "When I come home, most of the time I do my housework first, and at night I usually watch TV. When studying for a test, I don't watch TV. I use that time for extra studying."

GLO comment: Having time to relax at the end of a busy day is rewarding, but it appears that this student has been allowed flexibility for academic priorities.

Student C: "Studying has always been important and always stressed in our home. We had to do homework and studying first."

GLO comment: Every home and child will be different, but the completion of homework is necessary for a successful academic outcome. Parents have to value and demonstrate that time in their home for schoolwork is a priority. It is not enough to say it—this requires action. Make it a central focus and teach children how to be responsible for their own actions. Decide together on what time is preferred, then set up a quiet, comfortable study area with supplies available, and determine what the focus for the study time will be. If necessary, try several after-school options to see what works best.

There may be challenges, and the homework process might not flow as smoothly at homes that don't have sufficient time, resources, or support systems. But the attitude of both parent and student will make an enormous difference in the process and outcome. Homework should be approached positively and seen as an opportunity to learn new information that will be building blocks to a goal.

3) How do your parents help you stay focused on education?

Student A: "When I'm in school, I do my work. When I go home, I talk with my mom if I have any problems. She will tell me what to do in school to keep my grades up."

    GLO comment: The key theme here is that academic achievement action called *love*. Students work harder and perform better when they know that someone cares. The ideal situation is when parents take a leadership role in education.

Student B: "My grandmother has always had a positive influence on me, but they [my parents] increased their interest and help. They want to know everything I am doing. Every day they ask me what I did in school, what I did to make my grades come up. I started studying more and doing extra work. I started reviewing on my own and began asking teachers questions. Before, I would be afraid to ask a question, thinking the class and my friends would think it was stupid."

    GLO comment: Without a doubt, children really do depend on grandparents for guidance and to help them stay focused academically. This trusting relationship is enhanced with open communication and having clear family values, rules, and consequences.

Student C: "My mentor is someone I can confide in. If I can't talk to my mom about something, I call her. When I have a problem I cannot work out, she helps me. I do my internship at her school, and we have even more time together. She interacts with my family, like when my grades went down. She came over and talked with my family and suggested things I should start doing."

    GLO comment: Support could come from Mom, Dad, a sibling, grandparents, someone in the tribe, a teacher, or a mentor.

Students feel better knowing that someone has a genuine interest in them, and they're motivated by the encouragement and support of others.

4) What really makes education worthwhile?

Student A: "It's important to help people for you to be a success."

GLO comment: The empathy expressed by this student can make a difference in the lives of others. My guess is that this student's career choice will be in health care, education, counseling, pastoring, or some other helping profession.

Student B: "To help other people, because a lot of people have helped me as I have grown up."

GLO comment: It is always refreshing to hear students voice a desire to help others as a reason that makes education worthwhile. They learn a lot more than they realize during their educational pursuit. In addition to the core academic subjects of reading, writing, English, math, science, and social studies, schools teach much more. The valuable life skills of decision making, critical thinking, and problem solving are also gained during the pursuit of education. Personal development skills such as self-control, organization, communication, time management, and resiliency are additional benefits earned during an educational pursuit.

Student C: "I just like to stretch my mind and see what I can discover."

GLO comment: Taken from Sydney J. Harris's *Passion for Teaching*: "You can teach a student a lesson for a day; but if you can teach him to learn by creating curiosity, he will continue the learning process as long as he lives."

CHAPTER 15

Parent-Student Summary

Those participating in the survey from the Young Scholars Program without a doubt viewed education as a major priority. Families shared long-range educational goals that began with high expectations. Parents expected leadership, avoidance of negative peer pressure, above-average grades, and other indications of a desire to pursue excellence. The students in this group reflected these high expectations in their own goals for the future. They aspired toward careers that will lead to upward mobility.

These families reported that spiritual values served as a guide to everyday life and the foundation of their family values. Families placed a high priority on church attendance and regular active participation. Church was the place where young people witnessed acceptable behavior, were observed to see if they mimicked that behavior, and were corrected if need be. These students had a common and sincere desire to help others and to share both resources and knowledge.

The parents interviewed took a proactive approach to engaging their children in conversations about home, friends, school, personal achievements, challenges, and other topics that could affect their child's schoolwork. These parents appear to have established a gentle, interactive environment that encourages mutual conversation, rather than a controlling home, as they attempt to make learning fun. The students appear to have a more comfortable relationship with their mothers, mainly because of their accessibility, and rely more on them as a source of support.

The approach to homework varied among the students and the parents, but one common theme was that homework was done every day. Parents shared different strategies for checking homework, which included reviewing it together with the student and separately. Most parents kept an open ear and valued frequent discussion. Flexibility was permitted, depending on the preference and age of the child. As the children grow older, they take on more responsibility to get their work completed independently.

Students shared various schedules and preferences for homework, which included eating right after school, taking a nap before homework, watching television sometimes, talking on the phone, doing chores first, and doing homework late at night. The common theme, however, was homework every day. Discipline was nonnegotiable to keep students focused and achieving their academic goals. It was a key factor, not to be discarded.

In summary, establish a foundation based on generating learning opportunities that include family values lessons that teach respect, dependability, responsibility, self-sufficiency, assertiveness, and a strong work ethic. Practice academic achievement actions in your home that transparently and effectively demonstrate love, open communication, high expectations, parental involvement, and the importance of daily homework.

Students who are adequately prepared for the future understand the importance of family values early in life, demonstrate commitment and a willingness to sacrifice, and consistently achieve their academic goals. Families should begin where they are now and incorporate family values into their lives, making the necessary adjustments as children grow. It is never too late to start taking actions that support and lead to a high-achieving, competitive, successful life.

CONCLUSION

My goal in writing this book is for the words, people, stories, and information to serve as a frequent reminder that family values with actions lead to academic achievement. My hope is that my story will engage and empower students, parents, families, educators, and communities toward powerful relationships that are continuously generating learning opportunities. Family values and the actions that influence academic achievement must be positive and consistent. The education of children is so very important, and we must all engage and empower the children in our families, neighborhoods, cities, states, and country.

The five Watkins siblings—W. D. Jr., Glo, Ronnie, Cine, and Kay—reside in cities from Florida to Hawaii. What educational pathway would we each take? Attending college was an expectation, but each sibling took a different educational and career pathway and found personal success in their own way.

W. D. Jr. mixed a US Air Force military career with a Bachelor of Science degree in Curriculum Development and Computer Programming.

While I was away at college, I learned that Ronnie joined the US Army and completed high school and a bachelor's degree while enlisted. He was stationed in Hawaii, where he has made the blue skies, warm weather, and sandy beaches his home.

Lucine was gainfully employed immediately after high school and continued her rewarding business career in Atlanta, Georgia.

Our youngest sister, Sandra Kay, took yet another path as a young mom. She was employed for a while in Akron, relocated to Florida, enrolled in the US Navy reserves, and built her career with the federal government. Sandra Kay struggled as a single parent with three boys, but she continues to inspire me each day with her deep, burning desire to reach her academic goals. She was the least expected to graduate from high school, but now has two master's degrees and is an ordained minister.

I wish I could say that we were perfect children who never got off track, but I cannot. What I *can* say, however, is that our family values always directed us back on course.

Parents must establish clear family values with the members of their family and give considerable energy and attention to making these values come alive in day-to-day life. Parent and caregiver involvement should include supporting and motivating children to grow into mature, secure, intelligent, upwardly mobile adults. Students must know that their parents believe in them and appreciate their efforts. All citizens in our multicultural world must have high expectations, give their best, and experience the power of forgiveness and love.

Never become too busy to parent, support, or encourage a child. Our every word, step, and action serves as a role model. As the editor of this book would say, "Be who you want your children to be."

During my career in the formal education system, I have seen many successful schools with students excelling in every subject matter. However, in some school districts, policies, procedures, and test scores have taken precedence over student instruction. Regular school attendance, bullying, crime, classroom management, safety, and lack of regular parent involvement are indeed major concerns.

All schools must regain the primary role of educator and take the position of helping to prepare students for epic education. I believe this is expedited by demonstrating positive, constructive family values that lead to successful outcomes and options.

If students are to adequately prepare for the future, family values and academic achievement actions must not only represent the family's desire for their children, but also include commitment, sacrifice, and consistency. Many families, educators, and The Ohio State University Young Scholars community are demonstrating that neither economic nor family structure is a barrier to high academic achievement. There is agreement that family values are the foundation of life. Most parents desire that their children achieve academically, and it's important to generate learning opportunities at every possible moment.

Family Values Lead to Academic Achievement

Respect
Dependability
Responsibility
Self-Sufficiency
Assertiveness
Strong Work Ethic

Actions That Support Academic Achievement

Love
Open Communication
High Expectations
Parental Involvement
Daily Homework

RESOURCES

Academic Achievement

ACT is the leading US college admissions testing company. www. act.org Child Care Aware of America is a national network of more than seven hundred childcare resource and referral centers in every state and most communities across the country. www.usa.childcareaware.org

CNN.com Parent + Family. The Center for Work Ethic Development is helping organizations and people build a strong work ethic. www.cnn.com/specials/living/cnn-parents

Family Education's goal is to make it easier for busy moms and dads to raise happy, healthy, engaged children at every age and stage. www.familyeducation.com

Free Ride to College is a guide to grooming your kids for a full academic scholarship. Freeridetocollege.com

Head Start: Early Childhood Learning and Knowledge Center promotes a joint federal approach to improve early childhood education and development. ECD includes the Offices of Child Care and Head Start and the Interagency Team. eclkc. ohs.acf.hhs.gov

Internet Essentials believes that everyone should have access to the opportunities made possible by having Internet service at home. Since 2011, Internet Essentials is their answer to helping close the digital divide. www.internetessentials.com/

Kaplan SAT and ACT courses, developed by a dedicated team of learning engineers, are designed to teach the best test-taking strategies and give confidence on test day. www.kaptest.com/college-prep

Learning Disability Association of America provides support to people with learning disabilities, their parents, teachers, and other professionals with cutting-edge information on learning disabilities, practical solutions, and a comprehensive network of resources. ldaamerica.org/support/new-to-ld

National Black Child Development Institute provides and supports programs, workshops, and resources for African American children, their parents, and communities in early health and education, health, elementary and secondary education, child welfare, and parenting. www.nbcdi.org

National College Access Network's mission is to build, strengthen, and empower communities committed to college access and success, so that all students, especially those underrepresented in postsecondary education, can achieve their educational dreams. www.collegeaccess.org

National Education Association's mission is to advance the cause of public education. www.nea.org

National Merit Scholarship Corporation's mission is to recognize and honor the academically talented students of the United States. www.nationalmerit.org

National PTA is a registered 501(c)(3) nonprofit association that prides itself on being a powerful voice for all children, a relevant resource for families and communities, and a strong advocate for public education. www.pta.org

National Society of High School Scholars goal is to recognize academic excellence among high-achieving students, deliver to them value and opportunity through membership, and inspire them to realize their potential. www.nshss.org

National Summer Learning Association is the only national nonprofit focused on closing the achievement gap by increasing summer learning opportunities for all youth. www.summerlearning.org

Parent Toolkit is a one-stop-shop resource developed with parents in mind. www.parenttoolkit.com/explore-your-toolkit

PBS Parents is focused on the role of parents in a child's education. www.pbs.org/parents/education

Project Appleseed is an advocacy organization that engages public schools and families by mobilizing millions of volunteers, building responsibility, and promoting accountability, both at school and at home. www.projectappleseed.org

PTO Today is the only company dedicated exclusively to providing a full suite of products, programs, and services to the entire K–8 school-parent group market. www.ptotoday.com/parent-involvement

Quest Bridge is a national nonprofit based in Palo Alto, California, that connects the nation's most exceptional, low-income youth with leading colleges and opportunities. www.questbridge.org

SAT College Board is a mission-driven, not-for-profit organization that connects students to college success and opportunity. www.collegeboard.org

ThoughtCo believes that learning is a never-ending process and that great inspiration begins with a question. www.thoughtco.com/parent-role-in-education-7902

USNews.com. *U.S. News & World Report* is a multiplatform publisher of news and information. www.usnews.com/opinion/

articles/2016-09-30/how-parents-can-become-advocates-for-their-childrens-education

US Department of Education promotes student achievement and preparation for global competitiveness by fostering educational excellence and ensuring equal access. www2.ed.gov/parents/landing.jhtml

Young Scholars Program is a comprehensive, pre-collegiate and collegiate program designed to enhance the academic, personal, and career development of its scholars. odi.osu.edu/ysp

Personal Success

Administration for Children and Families, a division of the Department of Health and Human Services, promotes the economic and social well being of children, families, individuals, and communities with leadership and resources for compassionate, effective delivery of human services. www.acf.hhs.gov/

Be Your Best, by Dr. Patricia Larkins Hicks. Learn how to identify your assignment, develop it, and use your gift to be your B.E.S.T. www.amazon.com/Be-Your-B-S-T-enough/dp/145350284X

BusinessInsider is a business site with deep financial, media, tech, and other industry verticals. www.businessinsider.com/how-parents-set-their-kids-up-for-success-2016-4

Centers for Disease Control and Prevention increases the health security of our nation. www.cdc.gov

Center for Work Ethic Development is helping organizations and individuals build a work ethic. workethic.org/should-education-focus-more-on-soft-skills/

Child Development specializes in parent information, products, and services related to child development, psychology, health, parenting, learning, media, entertainment, and family activities, and strives to connect with other parents, professional experts organizations, and useful websites. www.childdevelopmentinfo.com

Family Voices aims to achieve family-centered care for all children and youth with special health care needs and/or disabilities. www.familyvoices.org

Girl Inc. inspires all girls to be strong, smart, and bold through direct service and advocacy. Their comprehensive approach to whole-girl development equips girls to navigate gender, economic, and social barriers and grow up healthy, educated, and independent. www.girlsinc.org

JumpStart is a 501(c)(3) tax-exempt nonprofit based in Washington, DC. As a coalition, they unite organizations committed to advancing financial literacy among preschool through college-age youth. www.jumpstart.org

Love and Logic Institute is dedicated to making parenting and teaching fun and rewarding, instead of stressful and chaotic. www.loveandlogic.com/parenting-for-success

Military Child Education Coalition is focused on ensuring high-quality educational opportunities for all military children affected by mobility, family separation, and transition. www.militarychild.org

National Center for Child Traumatic Stress (NCCTS). The National Child Traumatic Stress Network was established to improve access to care, treatment, and services for children and adolescents exposed to traumatic events. This section of NCTSN.org provides information about the network itself. www.nctsn.org/about-us/contact-us

Parenting Perspectives was founded on the belief that children and families will thrive in an environment of love, understanding, and connection. parentingperspectives.com/success-stories

Parenting Your Children into Adulthood, by Dr. Ron Hitchcock, presents a different perspective on how to form lifelong relationships with your adult children. www.lifeinmotionresources.com

Positive-Parenting-Ally is focused on powerful yet easy parenting and neatly captures founder Birgitte's parenting in general. www.positive-parenting-ally.com

Psych Central is the Internet's largest and oldest independent mental health social network. psychcentral.com/lib/category/parenting

Stop Wasting Your Time, by Tamara Hartley, includes fifteen life lessons to help take back control of your life, relationship, and career. www.YourHowToCoach.com

The Attached Family connects with children for a more compassionate world. theattachedfamily.com

The Learning Community is dedicated to providing the parenting resources and school help that parents need to lovingly, supportively, and successfully raise their children. www.thelearningcommunity.us

Verywell is a source for reliable, understandable information on hundreds of health and wellness topics. www.verywell.com

Wikihow is a worldwide collaboration of thousands of people focused on one goal: teaching anyone in the world how to do anything. www.Wikihow.com

Zero to Three's mission is to ensure that all babies and toddlers have a strong start in life. www.zerotothree.org

ABOUT THE AUTHOR

Gloria "Glo" Redding is the Founder/CEO and Education and Family Life Consultant of GLO: Generating Learning Opportunities. GLO is an expansion of her life commitment to engaging and empowering families, educators, and communities. She contributes years of wisdom, knowledge, and raw passion for family values and academic achievement.

Glo's candid perspectives based on her personal life journey, parenting style, professional experience, educational background, academic research, and her work in family advocacy are life changing. She proposes that many societal challenges can be addressed by establishing basic family values, which influence academic achievement and personal development. GLO provides inspiring custom designed and interactive trainings, speaking engagements, consultations and coaching services that focus on Academics, Family Values, Parenting and Personal Development.

The impactful sessions actively engage and empower clients with a trauma informed foundation.

Gloria is a graduate of The Ohio State University, where she earned a Bachelor of Science degree in Home Economics and a Master of Liberal Studies degree in Human Ecology. Glo is acknowledged as a National Council of Family Relations Emeritus Member and recognized by Who's Who. She is active with various ministries at Vineyard Columbus, is a life member of Delta Sigma Theta Sorority Inc., and serves on numerous community boards and committees.

She enjoys a spiritually, mentally, and physically balanced life with bible study, reading, sewing, Zumba, walking, and traveling. She resides in Columbus, Ohio and enjoys an active lifestyle with husband James, family and friends.

Visit the author's website at www.glolearning.com or email her at glo@glolearning.com.

ORDER TODAY

www.glolearning.com

- Personal autographed copies available upon request

- Discounts for bulk orders and when combined with other Generating Learning Opportunities services

  Contact GLO to schedule **GLO-Chat Book signings, consulting, training** or **speaking engagement** at *www.glolearning.com* or *info@glolearning.com*

  Join the GLO mailing list at *www.glolearning.com*

NOTES to Generating Learning Opportunities

NOTES to Generating Learning Opportunities

NOTES to Generating Learning Opportunities

Printed in the United States
By Bookmasters